ArtScroll Series®

Rabbi Nosson Scherman / Rabbi Meir Zlotowitz

General Editors

Mesorah Publications, ltd

Walking with Rabbi Miller

Daily Conversations
with an Inspirational Gadol

Rabbi Mordechai Dolinsky

FIRST EDITION
First Impression … October 2003

Published and Distributed by
MESORAH PUBLICATIONS, LTD.
4401 Second Avenue / Brooklyn, N.Y 11232

Distributed in Europe by
LEHMANNS
Unit E, Viking Industrial Park
Rolling Mill Road
Jarow, Tyne & Wear, NE32 3DP
England

Distributed in Australia and New Zealand by
GOLDS WORLD OF JUDAICA
3-13 William Street
Balaclava, Melbourne 3183
Victoria, Australia

Distributed in Israel by
SIFRIATI / A. GITLER — BOOKS
6 Hayarkon Street
Bnei Brak 51127

Distributed in South Africa by
KOLLEL BOOKSHOP
Shop 8A Norwood Hypermarket
Norwood 2196, Johannesburg, South Africa

ARTSCROLL SERIES®
WALKING WITH RABBI MILLER
© *Copyright 2003, by* MESORAH PUBLICATIONS, Ltd.
4401 Second Avenue / Brooklyn, N.Y. 11232 / (718) 921-9000 / www.artscroll.com

Cover photo courtesy of Tzemach Glenn

ISBN:
1-57819-378-8 (hard cover)
1-57819-379-6 (paperback)

Typography by CompuScribe at ArtScroll Studios, Ltd.

Printed in the United States of America by Noble Book Press Corp.
Bound by Sefercraft, Quality Bookbinders, Ltd., Brooklyn N.Y. 11232

Rabbi CHAIM P. SCHEINBERG

Rosh Hayeshiva "TORAH ORE"

and Morah Hora'ah of Kiryat Mattersdorf

הרב חיים פינחס שיינברג

ראש ישיבת "תורה אור"

ומורה הוראה דקרית מטרסדורף

בס"ד

ט"ז סיון תשס"ג

I would like to give my heartfelt ברכה to Rabbi Mordechai Dolinsky on his forthcoming book in which he shares his valuable insights and experiences gained from his precious walks with HaGaon HaTzaddik Rav Avigdor Miller zt"l who was one of the great luminaries of our generation, who spread the word of Hashem and the ways of the Torah to Clal Yisrael. I am sure that this book will be a source of inspiration to all.

May Rabbi Dolinsky be זוכה to have nachas from his family and to continue his work of הרבצת התורה להרבות כבוד שמים מתוך מנוחת הנפש והרחבת הדעת.

בברכת התורה והצלחה רבה,

RABBI YAAKOV HILLEL

Rosh Yeshivat

Hevrat Ahavat Shalom

45 Arzey Habira St. Jerusalem

יעקב משה הלל

ראש ישיבת

חברת אהבת סלום

רח' ארזי הבירה 45 ירושלים

בס"ד

ג' בחשון תשס"ג

דברי ברכה והמלצה

הריני בזה להמליץ על הספר "טיולים בפרדס" שחיבר ידידי הרה"ג כהר"ר מרדכי משה דולינסקי שליט"א. וענין הספר הוא, שבהיות הרב המחבר שליט"א בימי בחרותו, זכה להתלוות אל הגאון הגדול, זקן המשגיחים שבדורינו ורב רבנן בתורת המוסר, הנודע בעולם בספריו המלאים דעת יראת שמים והשקפה טהורה, ה"ה כמוהר"ר אבינדרב מילר זלה"ה, בעת הליכתו בדרך וטיוליו היום יומים. ותוך כדי ההזדמנות היקרה ללוות ענק רוח זה בדרכו בקודש, הבחין התלמיד בדרכיו והנהגותיו המופלאות, שהן נקודות אורה בתורה בהלכה ובמוסר, אשר ניתן ללמוד מהם דברים נפלאים ונסתרים ויחודיים בסדר עבודת העבד הנאמן לבוראו. ואותן רשם ופירש ונימק וביאר במוב טעם ודעת בבחינת "תלמיד המחכים את רבו", כדי להעביר ולמסור תורתו לדורות, תורת "ובלכתך בדרך".

והנה ספר מיוחד זה מצדיק הסכמה מיוחדת, ובפרט כי יש צורך להסביר תועלתו הגדולה.

אמרו חז"ל (ברכות דף ז' ע"ב): גדולה שמושה של תורה יותר מלמודה, ופירש הגר"א ז"ל (בספר חדושי וביאורי הגר"א לשם), שעל מנת לזכות להגיע למעלת אסוקי שמעתתא אליבא דהלכתא באמיתות, צריך יגיעה עצומה, וכמויות של חכמה ובינה ודעת במדות גדושות, כולי האי ואולי שבצירוף סייעתא דשמיא יזכה לכוין לאמיתה של תורה. אולם מי שזוכה לשמש תלמיד חכם גדול, הרי לומד ממנו מכל מעשיו ודיבוריו ותנועותיו תורה שלימה שכולה סולת נקיה להלכה ולמעשה, מה שאי אפשר היה להגיע אליה בכוחות עצמו אפילו על ידי העיון בספרים רבים, לולי השמוש לתלמיד חכם. ומסיבה זו רגיל אני לומר, שחיזוק מיוחד ורווחת הדעת מקבלים מהעיון בספר "מעגל טוב", שהוא יומן נסיעותיו של הגאון חיד"א ז"ל, כי מתוכו יתבונן ויבין המעיין איך אחד המיוחד מגאוני ישראל, התייחס לכל מיני מצבים וענינים שנפגש בהם, וסדר הנהגתו ותנובותיו ודיבוריו והרהוריו בכל מיני ענינים דקים וערינים, שהביע אותם ביחס למקרים שארעו לו למעשה. וזהי תורת אמת ממש, יותר אפילו מלימוד הלכה או לימוד מוסר מתוך ספרי הלכה וספרי מוסר, כי זוהי תורה למעשה ממש בסדר התנהגות האדם במקרים היותר פשוטים ותדיריים, לדעת השקפת תורה וסדר הנהגה בהם. וכן יש לומר על הספר הזה שמתבאר ממנו אופן קיום

הפסוקים: בכל דרכיך דעהו, ושויתי ה' לנגדי תמיד, ואל תפנו אל מדעתכם, ועניני זהירות נפלאים דקים ועדינים, בין אדם למקום ובין אדם לחבירו, כולם להלכה ולמעשה.

והנה מצד אחד אנו זוכים ללמוד מספר זה דרכיו והנהגותיו של אחד המיוחד מגדולי התורה והמוסר שבדורנו, המפורסם כעובד ה' אמיתי, אבל מאידך גיסא צריכים אנו לדעת כי בלי כשרונותיו ודעתו היפה והעמקיה של השותף לטיולים אלו בפרד"ס, שידע להבחין ולהבין ולהשיג הנהגותיו הדקות והעדינות של רבו, ולעמוד על טיבן ודיוקן, ולפרשן על נכון על פי יסודות המוסר וההלכה שבתו"ל, הרי לא היה יוצא הענין לפועל בהצלחה. כי מי שאין לו הכשרון להבחין נקודות דקות אלו, ולהבין לעומקן, ולדעת להסביר ולפרשן, לא היה עולה בידו להוציא מהם תורה שלימה למוסר והשקפה. ולכן בואו ונחזיק טובה לידידי הדגול הרה"ג כהר"ר מרדכי משה דזיונסקי שליט"א, שזוכה את הרבים בספר זה היקר, אשר המבקשים תורה ומוסר ודעת וסדר הנהגה אמיתי למעשה, יוכלו לדלות ממנו פנינים יקרים, ותן לחכם ויחכם עוד להתעלות בעבודת ה', כי היסודות שבהנהגות צדיק דגול זה ישמשו כמפתחות לפתוח עוד אוצרות רבים של תורה ודעת והשקפה נקיה.

ואסיים בברכה להרב המחבר שליט"א עוד כהנה וכהנה להגדיל תורה ולהאדירה, ולזכות את הרבים בשיעוריו המאלפים ובספריו החשובים. ויהי רצון שיזכה לאורך ימים ושנות חיים על התורה ועל העבודה מתוך בריאות איתנה ונחת וישוב הדעת וכל טוב לעד סלה אכי"ר.

הכותב והחותם לכבוד התורה ולומדיה

Dedication

I wish to dedicate this work to the memory of my dear parents—my father, Zelig *ben* Shmuel Dov Dolinsky, and my mother, Hadassah Ruchamah *bas* Chayim Dolinsky, *zichronam livrachah*—to whom I owe the sense of values that prepared me to feel the need to search for, find, and appreciate my Rebbe, Rav Avigdor Miller *zt"l*.

Considering the generation of which they were a part, and the fact that they lacked proper, direct input from Rav Miller himself, they should have found it quite impossible to relate to him and his ideas. Nevertheless they were supportive of my connection with him, and my father in the last years of his life proudly took the "big walk" to the Rugby section of Brooklyn for Rav Miller's afternoon *shiur* every Shabbos.

I have singled out my parents' wonderful supportiveness out of all the things for which I could praise them, because of its relevance to Rav Miller, the subject of this book. But in fact my parents were gems, sparkling with wonderful attributes, in particular that of being *ahuvim labrios,* beloved by all.

I am sure that my father and mother *a"h,* in their place in the World of Truth, will have much *nachas* from this work, especially since it is presented in their honor and blessed memory.

Table of Contents

Preface

The fine-tuned Torah mind combines with heart and soul to create insight that can process history and all that happens around us. This quality is not easily acquired and very difficult to find. My close friend and teacher, Rabbi Mordechai Dolinsky, is gifted with these qualities and is the most insightful person I know. When his depth is applied to even the most puzzling enigma, confusion becomes clarity and the heart rejoices.

Walking with Rabbi Miller is a book about the life and contribution of the legendary *gadol*, Rav Avigdor Miller. This book is not a biography or a historical treatment of an era. This volume is a Torah analysis of the master Torah analyzer. Rav Miller spoke such truth it was, at times, difficult to hear. But because it was truth, his words are eternal, his volumes are classics, and his life continues to be a beacon of light.

Walking with Rabbi Miller is a rare, in-depth peek into the mind and heart of a *gadol*, whom Reb Mordechai knew and understood so well. The book serves as an insight into the Almighty himself.

Walking with Rabbi Miller provides us with wisdom for life. Reb Mordechai embodies this wisdom and serves as a role model for all of us.

Rabbi Yaacov Haber

Acknowledgments

I would like to express my most sincere gratitude to all those who contributed to the production of this work:

The gifted and devoted ArtScroll staff for transforming this idea into a reality. I must make special mention of Mrs. Judi Dick who made important comments and revisions, Mrs. Mindy Stern who proofread and Devorah Scheiner who typeset the book.

My great appreciation to *HaGaon HaRav* Chaim Pinchas Scheinberg *shlita* and *HaGaon HaRav* Yaakov Hillel *shlita* for their warm, meaningful blessings and approbations.

Reb Shlomo Zalman Rappaport and his wife for their constant inspiration and encouragement.

Mrs. Yocheved Lavon for her deft and professional editing, and Mrs. Sarah Shapiro for her valuable advice and encouragement.

A *talmid* and *yedid* who prefers to remain anonymous, upon whom I can rely for anything and everything.

My dear wife for being at my side in every aspect, stage and issue. May the guidance and inspiration we received from the Rebbe through this work bring a multitude of blessings to her and to all those who contributed.

Introduction

I wrote this book as a memorial to *Rabi U'Mori*, Rav Avigdor Miller *zt"l*. I fervently hope it will serve as an inspiration and a source of enlightening insights to all who read it. To this end, I will share in these chapters many precious experiences, in particular the many walks I was *zocheh* to take with the Rebbe.

These walks took place during the years 5715 to 5725 (1955-1965). During this period the Rebbe was relatively unknown. It was then that he labored endlessly, tilling the earth, plowing the virgin soil, to effect a great metamorphosis in a community of laymen, while toiling simultaneously toward his own self-perfection and, in addition, working to elevate *bnei Torah* to true *bnei aliyah*. It was the golden period of the marvelous spiritual rebirth, growth, and blossoming of the Rugby community. This was the Rebbe's magnificent orchard which he cultivated with loving care until he had made it a unique, ideal, model Torah *kehillah*.

Today, most knowledge of the Rebbe, including a great part of his image and the impression he left, is based on recent observation and contact. The years from the 1970's through the 1990's, the years when the Rebbe was rising to prominence and at his peak of influence, are well known, and there are many who remember them. But there are relatively few (may they all live long and be well) who merited being in the Rebbe's inner circle during those early years. One of the benefits to be gained from this book is getting a glimpse of this vital era.

May Hashem grant healthy, happy years and much *nachas* to the Rebbetzin, who was dedicated to being the Rebbe's *ezer kenegdo* in every sense, and to his illustrious family, who represent the true continuation of his ideals.

May it be His will that the Rebbe's great merits bring *berachah* both spiritually and physically, to us and to all of *Klal Yisrael*.

CHAPTER ONE

How It All Began

Hashem's great gift to the world, *Mori V'Rabi HaRav Avigdor Miller zt"l* has been taken from us; it is an immeasurable loss for the world and for *Klal Yisrael*, and a personal loss as well.

Dear Rebbe,

You toiled to impress upon us what a difficult endeavor it is, and the obstacles one encounters in attempting to recount the life stories of those lofty souls, our great leaders in *Klal Yisrael*. Therefore I am certainly not going to attempt to portray *your* life. How unrealistic it is to think that one can actually capture and commit to writing the full dimension of true *ruchniyus*. Yet, I feel that I owe it to you and to *Klal Yisrael* to share a few rays of the great light in which I was privileged to bask for many years. Perhaps I shall realize this yearning by recalling certain experiences with you; perhaps I will manage to capture a peek, a glimpse …

As with countless multitudes in our generation, any appreciation for Torah, any connection that I have to it, indeed, all the fulfillment I have enjoyed, I owe to you. Your wisdom supplied me with what I needed to cope with the difficult challenges that unfortunately caused so many of my contemporaries to fall. In gratitude to the *hashgachas Hashem* that arranged this precious bond, I wish to relate the marvelous process of how this came to be.

In my early youth I lived in the Williamsburg section of Brooklyn. One of the cornerstones of Torah observance there in the 1940's and 1950's was the Young Israel of Brooklyn. This congregation was comprised of *baalei batim* who were actually great heroes for Hashem and the Torah. They were the standard-bearers of Torah, the pioneers who were totally responsible for the status Williamsburg eventually achieved as the most concentrated, intensive Orthodox Jewish neighborhood in all of America. This neighborhood underwent a complete tranformation, as it had previously been an irreligious area with every one of its businesses open on Shabbos. (I once heard an old-timer recall the days when the neighborhood had been completely gentile, with signs in the store windows proclaiming, "No Dogs or Jews Allowed.") The Shabbos observance of the Williamsburg community was achieved through peaceful, diplomatic demonstrations by the Young Israel members, which eventually influenced the owners to close their businesses on Shabbos.

Despite their heroism, these Shabbos-observant young people had grown up in a period in which a proper full-scale Torah education was regrettably unavailable. Raised in an era of extreme poverty, many had left yeshivah at a young age to supplement the family income. Unfortunately, they indeed fell short in their Torah knowledge. The community was, however, vivacious and inspired, with many organized activities for all ages. I can certainly say of my family that our lives centered around Young Israel. It was our source for all religious inspiration and the center of our social life. Those years provided a sense of tranquility, composed of the security of our extended family that surrounded us in Williamsburg, plus the support and inspiration we drew from the Young Israel community.

What I was not aware of was that I was actually on a collision course—despite my momentary peace of mind. I did not know that I was not properly equipped to cope with the challenges and problems that faced my generation. Despite the well-meaning high quality of the community, the growth of their religious life was stunted, for they lacked adequate nurturing for their spiritual advancement.

When survivors of the Holocaust began arriving in New York, they included many Jews who were rich in Torah and true service of Hashem. Because of the groundwork that had been laid by the Young Israel people, Williamsburg's reputation as a religious neighborhood attracted these immigrants. These new arrivals, inspired and imbued with Torah-true Judaism, had an extremely powerful influence on the general Jewish populace. Ironically, however, this influx had very little effect on most of the existing community. Secure in their *frumkeit,* they felt little need to seek inspiration from newcomers. In addition, radical cultural disparities in dress, language, social behavior, and general outlook alienated the immigrants from them.

My own personal period of utopia came to an abrupt and traumatic end when we were informed that a new highway was to be built—and it was to run right through the site of our house. Our happy, secure home was to be demolished. Strangely enough, our house was the only one on the block that would have to be knocked down to make way for progress. Forced to move, we somehow found ourselves in a new housing development in a section of Brooklyn between Crown Heights and East Flatbush, an area which at that time was largely undeveloped. I never quite understood why we did not resettle in Williamsburg. Be that as it may, in our new neighborhood I felt a desperate need to reconnect myself with Young Israel, and my research revealed that the nearest affiliate was the Young Israel of Crown Heights. Unfortunately, this was not within practical walking distance, at least not close enough to be my steady spiritual home. In the opposite direction there was another branch called the Young Israel of Rugby, and despite many attempts I failed to locate it. When I was finally successful in spotting the building I realized that my difficulty had been due to the modest size of the structure in comparison to the average Young Israel edifice. I tried *davening* there and was sorely disappointed; the service was not at all in the usual Young Israel spirit, which included lots of singing, and furthermore, there were no youth groups. When I commented about this to one of the congregants he replied that if I was looking for a conventional Young Israel, this was definitely not the place!

This was certainly a very trying period of my life. I was surrounded by a large spiritual void; there were many basic Torah issues that I found troubling and disturbing, and I had nowhere to turn for guidance or enlightenment. According to the Divine schedule the time was not yet ripe; I was not yet ready for the great light.

And then one day my older sister Ruth came home from school, her face shining. Someone had told her about a Rabbi ... A Rabbi? Where can he be found? ... At the Young Israel of Rugby.

Back I went, not looking for a Young Israel this time, but with an open heart and an open mind. When the Rabbi stood up and the words came forth from his mouth, I felt it was the first time I was being introduced to the *Ribono Shel Olam*.

CHAPTER TWO

Tzaddikim Yeilchu..., the Righteous Ones Walk

*A*fter making a comprehensive review of the years in which I gained so much from my Rebbe, it became apparent that I had numerous pivotal experiences that centered around the walks that we took together. I would like to share some of these experiences.

Most of these walks were in the framework of accompanying the Rebbe from shul to his home. There was a small group of us, an inner circle who were especially close to the Rebbe, and who usually accompanied him home after *davening* or *shiurim*. Every walk was a valuable learning experience. Generally, those who accompany a *talmid chacham* or Rebbe feel the need to make conversation. Often questions are asked just for the sake of asking. Alternatively, the disciple would expound on his own new insights in learning, or even just make small talk. We, however, were trained to be quiet when walking with the Rebbe (or for that matter in the company of anyone from whom we could learn) and to hope that the Rebbe himself would say something from which we could learn and grow. And so it was that as we walked, there would be absolute silence at the outset, until the Rebbe would come forth with a pearl of wisdom. Sometimes an "uninformed" stranger would join us and, to our great disappointment, would talk incessantly, and then the Rebbe would be politely quiet and not even try to get a word in edgewise. Usually, however, the Rebbe shared some thought, a *hashkafah*, an insight, or, what was most usual, he would quote a *pasuk* from *Mishlei*, accompanied by a beautiful explanation.

It is too bad that upon coming home each day I did not have the sense and appreciation to look up the *pasuk* and record the Rebbe's precious words. Basking in this light and being a recipient of these gems was my privilege week after week, month after month, year after year.

Before I relate my own experiences, let us take a glimpse at the role walking, which held a high priority in his day, played in the Rebbe's own life. He took this exercise with great consistency up until the very last days of his life, for at least forty to fifty years. The Rebbe began this activity when he was suffering from back discomfort. He was advised that walking would be greatly beneficial. This turned out to be sound advice, and the Rebbe always continued this practice.

For many years the Rebbe was *mashgiach* in Yeshivas Rabbeinu Chaim Berlin, then located in the Brownsville section of Brooklyn. After completing his day there he would walk several miles to his home in East Flatbush. My walks with the Rebbe were not in this framework; I generally accompanied him in our local neighborhood. When he left his position at Chaim Berlin, he continued his walking schedule with the utmost consistency, albeit following a different route.

It is essential to understand the implications of who and what we are dealing with here. The Rebbe was extremely careful regarding every second of his day. With the utmost seriousness he considered how and for what purpose he should use his time. The Rebbe, without any exaggeration, was probably one of the outstanding giants in our generation in this area. Because of the Rebbe's commitment to utilizing his time in the optimal way, he did not allow himself the luxury of vacations. The Rebbe did not attend weddings, even to fill the role of *mesader kiddushin*. The only *chasunos* he attended were those of his own grandchildren, and these on condition that they were held locally. Even at these, he participated only for a portion of time and this, with his coat draped over his arm throughout.

During the few hours of *shivah* that his sons sat for him here in *Eretz Yisrael*, some of the outstanding local *roshei yeshivos* and *manhigim* came to comfort the mourners. I personally heard them proclaim that the Rebbe was the *gadol hador* in *hasmadah* (devoting every available moment to Torah study) and safeguarding his time. It was also related that even as a *bachur* in Slabodka, the Rebbe had already earned a reputation as the outstanding *masmid* in the yeshivah!

Among his greatest life accomplishments were the *sefarim* he wrote and published. Every one is a monumental work. In *hashkafah* he wrote a complete ideology of the life of a Jew; he wrote on history, on *tefillah* and on the five *Chumashim*, the last volume on *Devarim* published shortly before his passing. There are also a great number of manuscripts as yet unpublished. At the *levayah* and the *shivah* something absolutely phenomenal was revealed. Due to his unrelenting commitment to his learning and the *shiurim* he gave, he never devoted more than 20 minutes a day to the writing of his *sefarim*.

When someone of such magnitude, who prioritizes every moment of his time, makes a commitment to taking daily walks, it is obviously noteworthy. The Rebbe did this within the framework of fulfilling the obligation to take care of one's body and guard one's health. This is certainly something from which we must all learn.

How did the Rebbe occupy himself during these walks, which consumed so much precious time? The following is just a sample: As mentioned above, for many years the Rebbe was *mashgiach* in

Yeshivas Chaim Berlin. Rav Hutner *zt"l* had invited him to fill this position in order to bring order and structure to the yeshivah. After completing his morning obligations as *mashgiach* the Rebbe would remain in the *beis midrash* for the course of the day. Some of the more inquisitive students could not contain their curiosity. Furtively, they would peek over his shoulder and see him focused on a certain *masechta* and *daf.* At the end of the day the "spies" observed that he had advanced ten *blatt.* Perhaps he was merely flipping through the pages. This pattern, however, was observed the next day, and the next and the next, week after week, month after month. Eventually it was clearly established that this was his regular learning program, ten *blatt* a day! Since this was discovered in an underhanded way, it was always considered the "spoken-about unspeakable," sort of a secret about the Rebbe that everyone knew. It really is amazing—the thought of someone maintaining such a *seder* on a consistent basis for years.

I once brought a *talmid chacham* to hear the Rebbe speak. Afterwards he remarked, "You can tell these words are coming from someone deeply familiar with *Shas.*" How right he was!

On one of our walks, the Rebbe described his regimen at length and in detail. What is relevant to us is this: The Rebbe described how he quickly learned through these ten *blatt,* but his program did not exclude *iyun,* delving in depth. Whenever he came across a difficulty he would write the question on a single index card and then place the card in his pocket. On his long walk home from the yeshivah he would take out the cards, and one by one, he would delve into the difficulty and contemplate different approaches to a solution. This was his activity for the walk during all those years in Yeshivas Chaim Berlin.

Toward the end of his life, the Rebbe revealed to those close to him that he had made a new decision. Instead of devoting his walking time to the preparation of a new book, he had decided to use the time to review *Shas* by heart. This was his last stage of preparation for the great test in the World to Come.

CHAPTER THREE

Miles and Miles

Dear Rebbe,

Aside from your many classes and numerous books, you have literally reached thousands through your cassettes. They range from renowned *roshei yeshivos* and noted *talmidei chachamim* to those who were totally disconnected from the Torah and its observance, many of whose souls were reignited through your inspiration.

Turning back the clock, I recall the 1950's as a time when my admiration for the gems that poured forth from you was at a peak. At the same time I was filled with overwhelming frustration at the thought that such a precious light of truth was relatively unknown to the world outside our community.

At that time, there was nothing at all from Rebbe that was recorded or written. Nothing. I was filled with an enormous yearning and ambition to see to it that his words should be documented for posterity. The Rebbe had not mentioned plans to publish any works, and as for recording, it was the dawn of the "reel-to-reel" era. Large and cumbersome, these early tape recorders were difficult to come by. But the greatest obstacle I had to overcome was the fact that the Rebbe was not giving any weekday *shiurim* during that period. So even if I could have gotten hold of a recorder, when would I be able to record him? There was the Friday night *Chovos HaLevavos*, the Shabbos morning *derashah*, and the Shabbos afternoon *Aggadata shiur*. Since most of the *baalei batim* were at work, they were not available at Minchah and Maariv time on weekdays. Therefore, there were no *minyanim* for these prayers at our local Young Israel other than on Shabbos. There was, however, a period during the summer when sunset was late enough to make a weekday afternoon *minyan* possible. The Rebbe took advantage of this opportunity to give a brief *shiur* in *Chovos HaLevavos* between Minchah and Maariv. I, too, wanted to seize this, my only opportunity to capture the Rebbe's golden voice and wisdom on tape, and I became obsessed with working toward this goal. I had a few months to orchestrate this delicate operation. First, I had to secure one of these bulky reel-to-reel tape recorders, which few people owned. After several months of grueling anticipation the summer arrived and I managed to get my act together. A relative who owned a tape recorder was willing to lend it to me, I arranged transportation, and, of course, I procured the Rebbe's approval. The assigned day finally arrived, and the ecstasy I felt cannot be described. I actually managed to record the Rebbe's voice, which was beautiful in both a physical and spiritual sense. I do not think the ownership of anything in the universe could have had more value to me. I was holding in my possession a piece of the Rebbe.

Then my ecstasy was shattered. It is impossible to describe my disappointment when the Rebbe informed me that due to certain remarks he had made during the *shiur* which he felt were not for general circulation, he wanted the tape destroyed. It was impossible to arrange the whole recording ordeal again that season, which meant waiting an entire year for another attempt. This was something that was impossible for me to contemplate.

Before continuing the story, I want to note that eventually, as compensation, the Rebbe offered to give a one-time, special *shiur* specifically for the purpose of this recording. After a group of close *talmidim* was organized, this special *shiur* became a reality. Today this remains the first recorded *shiur* by the Rebbe. A few months later the Rebbe was invited to be the guest speaker at the grand Chanukah Melave Malka of the Agudath Israel branch of the Washington Heights Congregation. I naturally grabbed this opportunity to once again record the Rebbe, and this very inspiring speech became the second recording of the Rebbe. I still have both of these original recordings in my possession.

It is well known that our *manhigim* are beneficiaries of an inordinate amount of *siyata d'Shmaya*, Divine help, which, I feel, borders on actual *ruach hakodesh*. There is a tendency among our leaders to hide this gift, and this was likewise the case with the Rebbe; however sometimes it shows through …

I wish to again bring to your attention that all this took place at the dawn of the reel-to-reel recording era, before cassettes were invented. Each single recording was a rarity. It was many years before anyone dreamed there would ever be the popular Thursday night class, which supplied the main material for the well-known cassettes.

During our walk home together from this "unrecorded" *shiur*, it was impossible for me to hide my crushed feelings. The Rebbe sensed my broken and disappointed spirit and attempted to comfort me. When we reached his home and were about to part for the evening the Rebbe looked me in the eye and said: "Mordechai, don't feel bad, some day there will be miles and miles of my tapes."

CHAPTER FOUR

"???"

*W*e who have learned Torah are accustomed to the importance of attributing all we have to Hashem *yisbarach*. The Rebbe taught us the importance of realizing that even the unbidden thoughts or ideas that occur are likewise from Hashem. A classic example is the well-known incident when Avimelech captured David HaMelech. David's death seemed imminent, with no apparent way for him to save himself. Then David HaMelech had a "brainstorm": he would act as if he had lost his mind. It worked—no one takes vengeance on a demented enemy. David HaMelech's gratitude to Hashem was overwhelming— he recognized that it was Hashem who had put the idea into his mind, and as a monument of his gratitude he composed Psalm 34. It is included in the *pesukei d'zimrah* we say every Shabbos morning—"*L'David b'shanoso es taamo lifnei Avimelech vayegarshehu* *vayelach*—Of David: When he disguised his sanity before Avimelech who drove him out and he left." With this as a background, I would like to relate the following episode.

In the late 1950's a mass demonstration took place in midtown Manhattan to uphold the honor of the Brisker Rav which had been degraded by some "Rabbi." Of course, the Rebbe attended. I remember sitting next to the Rebbe at that rally (he was seated in the audience with the *tzibbur*). Every time a speaker brought up an important point, the Rebbe would clap and bang his feet, which would start a chain reaction until the entire audience was cheering. This was very out of character for the Rebbe. What he was doing, however, was taking advantage of the opportunity to increase *kevod Shamayim*, the honor of Hashem.

When the rally ended, the Rebbe said that he was planning to walk home a good part of the way and invited me to join him. The route the Rebbe selected was a quiet, relatively empty side street instead of one of the crowded main avenues in Manhattan. As always on our walks, the Rebbe was discussing an important topic. He might have been giving me one of his insights regarding the demonstration or an explanation of a *pasuk* from *Mishlei*. This taste of *Gan Eden*, however was interrupted when we were approached by a "coat collar up and hands in pockets," underworld-looking individual, requesting a "donation." This character was dangerous, and it seemed highly likely that if a wallet were to appear he would promptly grab it and run away. On the other hand, if we refused him he might turn violent. The prospect of outrunning him did not seem promising or practical; this was what they call a "catch-22" situation.

A sort of paralysis took hold of me; I froze in my place—not having the slightest inkling of what to do. I was also getting the feeling that the "gentleman" was becoming a little impatient. The Rebbe then broke the silence, saying something that I thought I was not hearing correctly. The character again made his request. This time I heard what the Rebbe said, but I did not understand a word of it. Again the request was repeated by the obviously agitated interloper.

The Rebbe again presented his answer, this time louder and clearer but completely incomprehensible.

What *was* the Rebbe saying? Although I do not pride myself on being a linguist, there is a certain familiarity we all have with the most common languages. We have at least some recognition of French, Spanish, Italian, German, Hungarian, Russian, Polish, Arabic, even Chinese — but this phrase did not sound even close to anything I could recognize. I wondered if it was some secret Kabbalistic uttering. Most amazing of all was the Rebbe's composure. I was nervous as could be, yet the Rebbe was completely relaxed, making this strange utterance without any indication of anxiety or tension. He even said it with a smile!

This frightening exchange kept bouncing back and forth, the thug becoming more and more annoyed each time while the Rebbe kept calm, answering in a natural conversational tone of voice. The man, realizing that he had no way of communicating, looked at us, shrugged his shoulders, and went on his way. What a close call! I was trying to regain my composure and assess what had just taken place.

The Rebbe sort of poked me and signaled that we remove ourselves from the location. For the rest of that walk we "honored" the main thoroughfare with our presence. The Rebbe continued from where he had left off before the rude interruption, and I waited impatiently for a lull in the conversation so I could ask for an explanation of what had just transpired. As soon as my opportunity came, the Rebbe explained that while he was learning in Slabodka as a *bachur* he would hike on the mountainside during *bein hazmanim* vacation. What I had heard was a rare Lithuanian dialect that he had picked up in the back hills during these excursions.

The Rebbe then explained that he had refrained from using any other conventional foreign language as he could not know with what language the "gentleman" might be familiar. One thing was certain, though—he would not know this obscure Lithuanian dialect. An absolute brainstorm—and it all came as quick as a flash. The Rebbe emphasized the need for us to acknowledge that the inspiration for this tactic had come from Hashem, and how much praise and thanks we owed to Him.

CHAPTER FIVE

Rabbi, You Have a Good "Pointer" There!

One of the *hashkafos* the Rebbe spoke about was how one should deal with the verbal abuse that Jews, especially religious Jews, are sometimes subjected to. There is a certain mind-set that is part of Jewish pride and human self-respect, which dictates that these insults or physical annoyances must not be taken "sitting down." Many consider it a holy duty to protect the honor of our nation, or their personal pride, by demonstrating an aggressive reaction. The Rebbe spoke out strongly against this. He pointed out how foolish it is to become embroiled in conflicts that may have dangerous consequences as a result of a few senseless insults. "Just ignore it and continue on your way" was his advice and outlook. The Rebbe's attitude in this regard also pertained to Jewish organizations and groups that preach aggressiveness and violence.

Another important principle that the Rebbe often spoke about was the concept of rational flexibility and adaptability. There is almost no principle, despite its truth and importance, that is universally applicable.

It was summertime, *bein hazmanim*. Yeshivas Chaim Berlin was not in session, and in place of his daily walk home, the Rebbe chose very early morning for his regular walks. I had decided to remain in the city this *bein hazmanim*, and so I accompanied him daily. As usual, the Rebbe was in the course of sharing his insights on a *pasuk* from *Mishlei* with me. (Again, as I write, I feel regret over the great loss that I did not commit these lessons to writing upon arriving home.)

The early morning air was fresh and invigorating. At this hour many of the local stores and supermarkets had their workers bringing in and arranging the merchandise. Suddenly I was startled; the Rebbe had stopped speaking. Then I realized that he was no longer at my side and I was walking alone. I turned and witnessed the following scenario: We had just passed a large supermarket and a group of burly employees were working outside. One of the crew was especially tall and broadly built. The Rebbe had moved from the sidewalk and was standing right opposite this big fellow, face to face. Whereupon the Rebbe stuck out his finger right at him; it looked as though it was going to penetrate right through the man's face. The fellow looked quite overwhelmed and shocked, not really expecting this. "Keep your mouth shut," said the Rebbe to him in a stern voice, "and don't you ever say that again." The Rebbe then gave him a stern look and with that, he walked away. Obviously the fellow had made some nasty, derogatory remark. As we continued our walk, the Rebbe explained that he felt that as a Rav in the community, he had a special responsibility to put this person in his place for what he had said.

To really appreciate this episode one must understand how strongly the Rebbe always criticized the "nobody is going to start up with me" mentality. Often the Rebbe pointed out the senselessness of getting involved in such situations and expressed the view that one should rather quietly back off and leave the scene.

It is also interesting to contemplate how much inner strength is required to stand up to someone of such physical stature.

This episode is an outstanding demonstration of the flexibility/adaptability outlook. Even if one feels strongly about an issue, one should work to develop the sensitivity to discern where the principle is not applicable and use his discretion accordingly.

CHAPTER SIX

Who Cut Down This Cherry Tree?

One of the topics the Rebbe spoke about and instructed us in was the importance of uplifting the spirits of others. This includes restoring the spirits of someone who is down, as well as lifting even higher someone who is up.

The Rebbe was once riding in a van with R' Moshe Feinstein *zt"l* and a group of *bachurim*. When R' Moshe was let off at his destination the Rebbe started singing a lively *niggun* and clapping his hands. Immediately all the boys joined in. This was totally out of character for him. Afterwards the Rebbe explained his puzzling behavior. The Rebbe had noticed that there was one boy in the group whose spirit was especially down, hence he had made the little impromptu "*kumzitz.*" I was once likewise the recipient of this magnanimous form of *chesed*.

It was summer vacation time. The Rebbe invited me to join him on his walk. The Rebbe concluded a conversation with one of his *baalei batim,* who handed him a large, important-looking manila envelope. They parted, and we were off on our evening promenade.

As usual, the Rebbe expounded on a *pasuk* in *Mishlei*. The route he selected kept gravitating toward deserted side streets. We eventually found ourselves in a really desolate area and there, the Rebbe paused at a small alcove, at the entrance to a store. At this hour the store was already closed, so the spot was quite private. He stopped and looked back and forth to make sure no one was around. He then took the important-looking manila envelope from under his arm, squeezed the metal clips together and proceeded to open the envelope. He put his hand in and out came the most beautiful, fresh, red cherries! The Rebbe then informed me that the man he had been conversing with earlier had a cherry tree in his backyard and had presented this sampling to him. The Rebbe held out a sprig of gleaming fruits and invited me to join him in indulging in these luscious-looking specimens. At that point he brought up an issue mentioned in the *gemara*: *Ha'ocheil bashuk domeh l'kelev*—Partaking of food in a public place is considered degrading and is looked upon with disdain. He then went on to a short *pilpul*, pointing out a halachic leniency that could be applied in our case.

You must understand that we had a tremendous *yiras hakavod* (awe and respect) for the Rebbe, and although offering me some cherries was certainly a beautiful gesture on his part, I felt uncomfortable and self-conscious. But the Rebbe insisted, and the cherries were as delicious as they looked.

How's that for lifting someone's spirit? It was a miracle I didn't fly into space.

CHAPTER SEVEN

Big Things Come from Little Walks

*F*riday evenings with the Rebbe forty to forty-five years ago were quite busy. As was the style then, after the *seudah* there would be a *derashah* for the congregants. Following the *derashah* most of the *kehillah* would leave. Next was a *shiur* in *Chovos HaLevavos*, which was attended by a smaller group. In the last years, the Rebbe's *Chovos HaLevavos shiur* had a large attendance. But in those days the Rebbe was not so well known and we had him to ourselves. After the *Chovos HaLevavos shiur* many people left and yet a smaller group of closer *talmidim* remained to accompany the Rebbe home. The walk home, as previously noted, was in reality another brief *shiur*.

When we arrived at the Rebbe's home the closest *talmidim* accompanied him inside, and we would sit around the dining room table. The Rebbetzin, she should live and be well, served refreshments. Just to be sitting in these surroundings, basking in the warmth and presence of the Rebbe, was *me'ein Olam Haba*—like a taste of the Next World. When we first entered and sat down there was always silence in the room. This silence had a double significance. First, it was part of a general deportment that the Rebbe taught: when in the presence of a Rav or a great *talmid chacham*, one should allow him the initiative to open the conversation. Second, the Rebbe taught us that people should train themselves to be able to enjoy being in the company of their acquaintances, relatives, or loved ones without necessarily engaging in conversation. The Rebbe provided us an opportunity to practice this.

Eventually the Rebbe would break the silence, sometimes sharing some new insight with us. Most often, he would select an *Aggadata* from a *gemara*, usually a *Chazal* that needed an explanation in order to make even its basic meaning accessible. Then he would ask for our interpretation. Those who had something to offer would speak up. The Rebbe would listen and make his comments. What an opportunity for growth! The Rebbe would actually listen attentively to our explanations and comment on them.

In the late 1950's a black leather jacket was a status symbol for a certain prototype of a ruffian, a pseudo-gangster. On one particular Friday night we were walking home: One of our intimate group had once encountered an irreligious young Jew on the street and had made an effort to strike up a conversation with him. He had succeeded in establishing an initial contact with him. Now, as we walked, he noticed this fellow in passing and signaled him to come join us. This young man was very much involved in sports and body-building. His muscular build was very obvious. Why he agreed to come along with us was puzzling—but there he was—black leather jacket and all, together with the "inner circle group." The Rebbe, who was in the midst of saying a *d'var Torah*, indicated his approval at having the young man join us. As we approached the Rebbe's home, an invitation to come up to the house was extended to him, too. What is amazing is that the Rebbe was willing to have him join us even though he was light-years away from this group and from what we were engaged in. It was as though an angel was guiding the Rebbe to do so. Although he stuck out like a sore thumb, nevertheless he sat down with us, "the knights of the round Torah table." The initial quiet period was too much for him, and at a certain point he found it difficult to contain himself. However, this first experience of being accepted by the Rebbe and the group set in motion a sequence of events that resulted in his slowly coming to observe the Torah. Even though I was personally involved in his "*kiruv*," I eventually lost contact with him.

In Yerushalayim, many years later, when I was *mashgiach* in Yeshivas Torah Ore, a dignified-looking gentleman dressed in a homburg and frock coat approached me before Maariv and asked if we could speak after *davening*. It was not difficult for me to guess what he wanted. A trend was starting; up until then, the *roshei yeshivah* in *Eretz Yisrael* had been attempting to attract *bachurim* from the U.S. to their respective yeshivos. Most of the boys from the U.S. would come for a year or two and then return to continue their learning in the States. Now, *roshei yeshivah* from the States were coming to *Eretz Yisrael* to familiarize the heads of yeshivos there with their institutions so that they could direct students their way. My guess was correct; this dignified-looking guest was indeed a *rosh yeshivah*. He skillfully presented a detailed profile of his yeshivah, outlining their approach to learning, methods of dealing with the boys, and the type of *bachurim* they accommodated. At the end of this pleasant conversation, he was about to leave. I had a nagging feeling that I knew him from somewhere, but I had no inkling from where. I told him he seemed somehow familiar to me, so we went down the check list together—the yeshivos we had learned in, the places we had lived, the camps we had gone to; but we uncovered no hint. Then, suddenly, it hit me—the homburg peeled away, the frock coat peeled away, the neatly trimmed beard peeled away, forty years peeled away. Richie! There he was, sitting before me in his black leather jacket. Richie—the *rosh yeshivah*. We kissed, reminisced, and relived that special Friday night, and then he filled me in with a brief account of how he had gotten to where he was today.

Big things come from little walks.

Sequel: More Big Things From Little Walks

Some years later, the son of our above-mentioned *rosh yeshivah* was in *Eretz Yisrael*, a young man in his early 20's. He was having some difficulties and I was approached to help him. A few attempts were made to arrange for us to meet, but somehow they never materialized. One Shabbos I was headed to the *Kosel* through an unfamiliar neighborhood. I met a young man and asked him if he was familiar with the way. It turned out that he was an American, likewise on his way to the *Kosel*, and likewise not quite sure of the way. We joined forces. In the course of the conversation, as we walked, he mentioned that his father was the head of a certain yeshivah. You guessed it. He was that son that I had been trying to reach. And so we made contact in a very casual way, and as a result we fixed a time to meet and eventually developed a close tie.

As I said, big things happen from little walks.

CHAPTER EIGHT

About-Face

What I am about to share in this chapter is perhaps one of the most revealing and enlightening conversations I ever had with the Rebbe. I have a strong suspicion that this might have been the only time he revealed this, and it is something that proved to be of great benefit for many.

There is a famous *Chazal* that tells about a *Tanna*, Shimon HaAmsani, who devoted himself to a lifetime project. He was of the opinion that anywhere in the Torah that the word את, *es,* is mentioned, there is a connotation that something additional is being alluded to. He then undertook the massive project of finding every occurrence of the word *es* in the Torah and deriving its meaning; that is, what additional thing was referred to in each particular verse. When he came to the word *es* in conjunction with Hashem, he felt that he was stymied. Since G-d's Name could not possibly include anything else, this instance showed that his whole premise was flawed. He admitted defeat, rejected his hypothesis entirely, and retracted all the work he had invested. (R' Akiva claimed that the *es* in conjunction with Hashem came as a hint that *talmidei chachamim* were included in the mitzvah given in the verse.)

The Rebbe elaborated on this *Chazal* often, pointing out the greatness of this *Tanna,* who had lectured on his theory and invested considerable time and energy. Yet after all that, having the honesty and thirst for truth to recognize it, he admitted his error, changed his mind, and retracted his whole premise.

I will always remember how, the very first time I heard the Rebbe speak, the topic of *Olam Haba* came up. I was overcome by a very unusual reaction. *Baruch Hashem*, I came from a religious family and had attended yeshivah my whole life. Nevertheless, upon hearing the Rebbe speak about this subject I was overcome with a feeling that this was the first time I had heard it dealt with in a manner which conveyed that the next world is a true reality. There were actually such things as *Olam Haba* and *Gehinnom*! The Rebbe also pointed out that the subjects of *Olam Haba* and *Gehinnom* are generally treated very lightly, and that if one just mentions these topics he is sure to get a big laugh out of his listeners. It was as a result of this *derashah* that I was attracted to the Rebbe; I felt that I was basking in an aura of *divrei emes*. I was overcome with a sense of spiritual commitment, a feeling that I must make a connection with this person from whom such truth was emanating.

Many years later, in the 1970's, I had already been living in *Eretz Yisrael* for a number of years, away from the Rebbe, and I took a trip to the States for a short stay. I had been offered a postion and I called the Rebbe for an appointment to discuss some question I had. The Rebbe was scheduled to speak at a yeshivah a half-hour's walk from his home. He invited me to accompany him. When I arrived the Rebbe informed me that his speech had been canceled, but we could walk near his home instead. I now had the advantage of not being limited by the time parameter of reaching the yeshivah as we had originally planned. As it turned out, we walked for several hours up and down the block of his house. It was by far the longest walk with the Rebbe I ever was *zocheh* to, and it was the longest single conversation I ever had with the Rebbe. It was also the most revealing. I do not think we had ever had a conversation before in which the Rebbe was so open and candid about himself, how he felt about certain life decisions he had made, and about his accomplishments.

The discussion revolved around my accepting the position and the potential amount of Torah learning that would be available to me if I did so. Since it was relevant to the matter at hand, the Rebbe brought up a subject that I had never heard him discuss or even refer to. For many years the Rebbe had followed a program of learning many *blatt* of *gemara* every day, as was described above (see Chapter 1). This was something that was discreetly discovered by some aggressively curious students. Now, for the first time, I actually heard the Rebbe speak about his learning schedule.

He described to me how he had developed a system of learning ten *blatt* daily, day after day, how he had accomplished this with the utmost consistency and diligence. He explained that it was all done within a tight schedule to which he kept meticulously. "I remember walking home from Yeshivas Chaim Berlin and standing on such and such a street, and making an inventory with myself to see if I was on schedule with where I should be holding. Many people have attempted such programs but were unable to carry them through as I did."

This program and system seemed like a Utopia; all that was missing was an element of *iyun*, devoting time for logically analyzing and intellectually dissecting the *gemara*. The Rebbe then explained that his *seder* was not only *bekius*, a ground-covering program. Whenever a question arose, it was written down on a single index card. At the completion of each day of working and learning in the yeshivah, the Rebbe walked home from Brownsville to East Flatbush as described above. During these extensive daily walks, he would take out these index cards, and one by one he would deal with the questions, intensively searching for possible solutions until he felt satisfied that the subject was exhausted, and then go on to the next card. In revealing to me his personal system and accomplishment, the Rebbe was describing an ideal program.

Then the Rebbe continued: "*Ashrei mi sheba v'talmudo b'yado*—Fortunate is he who arrives with his learning in hand." The goal is for a person to come to the next world with his Torah learning internalized. One must have what is called a *kinyan* on his learning—he must completely "acquire" it; one must make it a part of himself. "True, having such a program of going through the whole *Shas* many times is the greatest of accomplishments ... However," said the Rebbe, "I have come to the conclusion that a more realistic and reliable method of assuring a substantial *kinyan* is by giving an *iyun shiur*, transmitting the Gemara to others on a high intellectual level—delving ... analyzing ... intellectually dissecting. The idea of *talmudo b'yado*, coming to the next world with true Torah accomplishments, is a very pressing business, and it must be taken seriously."

Here was a major turnabout. In the past the Rebbe would advise his students to invest their learning efforts to cover ground and complete many *mesechtos*, believing that this was the mark of someone whose learning is sincerely oriented to becoming knowledgeable in Torah. Now he was changing his whole perspective and advising me to make a priority of being familiar with the material that would make me eligible for a position as *maggid shiur*. In the long run, it is this that affords the opportunity to make a real *kinyan*, to acquire and truly internalize the Toras Hashem.

The Rebbe then stated, to my shock and surprise, that he regretted the whole system he had pursued. How much better would it have been if he had taken the route of becoming a *maggid shiur*, if he had made an effort to attain a position in which he could give a high level, in depth, *gemara* class.

He then added: "If you don't have new wood available to build a *succah*, you use old doors." Now that he had missed the opportunity, the Rebbe said, he would at least use what was available to him toward this goal of making a *kinyan* through teaching the *baalei batim*.

The inspiration and insight I received from the Rebbe that day, to appreciate the opportunity to give an *iyun shiur*, I shared with others. On a number of occasions I encountered people who had been offered the chance to give an *iyun shiur* and were hesitant, or who held such a position and were considering leaving. They were lacking an understanding of the important ramifications of the position's effect on their own *kinyan haTorah*, on which I was able to enlighten them. Likewise, there were situations where people had the opportunity to organize their own *shiur*, which I encouraged them to do, based on this inspiration from the Rebbe.

Shimon HaAmsani would surely be proud and have *nachas* from the Rebbe's exhibition of such strength in letting go of a tremendous past investment and making a complete about-face. How well this fits in with the way the Rebbe dealt with the eternal life as a complete reality. *Ashreinu she'ra'inu*—how lucky we were to have seen.

CHAPTER NINE

Showers and Flowers

The word used in *lashon hakodesh* for all material goods and objects is *gashmiyus*. The reason is that almost every physical object in the world has its source, directly or indirectly, in *geshem*, rain. It is fascinating to investigate just how everything traces back to rain. There is a strongly negative attitude toward rainy weather that prevails in our Western society. How often do we see examples of the popular secular culture featuring rain as a metaphor for sadness or bad luck?

The day darkness fell upon the world, the day that *Klal Yisrael* and the whole world suffered the loss of the Rebbe, he had a lengthy conversation with his older son, Eliezer, from his hospital bed. It was replete with instructions and personal matters. R' Eliezer personally related to me that the Rebbe told him that if he wanted to be happy in life, he should learn the *sefer Chovos HaLevavos*. The Rebbe then added that if he wanted to be even happier, he should include the

Mesillas Yesharim. Chovos HaLevavos is a *sefer* of *mussar*, *chizuk*, and *yiras Shamayim*. What did the Rebbe mean about attaining happiness from learning the *Chovos HaLevavos*?

Chovos HaLevavos teaches us to examine and evaluate Hashem's creation with an open and objective eye in order to perceive the inherent goodness therein. This *sefer* contains principles of life and attitudes of thought that will bring true joy to one who adopts these perspectives. The Rebbe explained that if a person would stop to consider what is actually transpiring on a rainy day, he would see that anything and everything he desires, from his most basic needs for life sustenance to the luxuries he wishes for, is in the making!

How could a person with the proper perspective not look positively on what is transpiring when it rains? How could there be a trace of negativity at being the recipient of blessings? How can we grumble at the treasures showering down upon us?

In my memory I am walking with the Rebbe, and dark, "threatening" clouds in the distance are closing in on us. Before you know it we feel actual precipitation, intermittent and gentle at first, then turning into a very wet downpour. All this is marked by an increase of action on the street, people running helter-skelter and being very vocal with their complaints. We continue walking together, and the Rebbe changes the topic and addresses the subject of the raindrops. He focuses on the vegetation, the colorful, flavorful fruits that we enjoy and indulge in, and explains that they are actually "coming down" right now in the form of raindrops. Then he continues to enumerate other gifts of Hashem, including the wonderful world of *sefarim* that are in the making at this moment, as they are printed on paper that grows in the forest. He then points out that "people" are falling: all the new babies, our own children and grandchildren—*Klal Yisrael*, the *tzaddikim!*

Now to see the Rebbe's face—the joy, the excitement and ecstasy. A person in need is pelted with thousands of golden nuggets. It is one thing to sit in a dry, comfortable home, lecturing about the wonderful blessings of rain, repeatedly verbalizing this concept. But to be out in the wetness of the rain pouring down, and then to be in a state of ecstasy, certainly reflects one's true feelings.

What we have just seen is a sample of *simchas hachaim*, the joy of living, from the *sefer Chovos HaLevavos*. This *sefer* is eye-opening and head-straightening. If one learns it properly (which is not a simple matter), delves into the ideas it presents and works to make them an integral part of himself, and then devotes himself to apply its lessons to life, it will bring him true joy. The Rebbe was a prime example of this. (In general, one could see the principles the Rebbe taught exemplified in his life.) It was not just the joy of walking in the rain. This incident was symbolic of how the "*Chovos HaLevavos* joy" studded his entire life. This was probably the secret of the Rebbe's "fountain of youth." The passing of years was almost indiscernible on him. True, the Rebbe was very strict about *hilchos bri'us*, his personal health care; he always ate wisely and took his daily walks; but it was his *simchas hachayim* that kept him youthful in looks and action.

The principle that we dealt with here, which the Rebbe taught us, of examining, evaluating, and recognizing the good in what is generally thought of as otherwise, is perhaps among the primary axioms of life and happiness.

CHAPTER TEN

Blessed Blessings

ashem said to Avraham: "*Heyei berachah*—Be a blessing," and with that a special power of blessing was given to Avraham and his progeny. The mechanism of *berachah* is a specific force that brings abundance, growth, expansion, and longevity. The power of *berachah* is accessed by the spoken word intensified with mental concentration. By saying the words of the *berachah*, we bring the blessing. It is equivalent to pushing buttons and tapping into special powers that Hashem created.

All this is not to be confused with *tefillah*, prayer, through which we also exercise influence and have input on the universe, albeit through a different mechanism and other channels than those accessed by *berachah*. In *tefillah* we make an appeal, petition, and request to Hashem. The Rebbe opened our eyes to new dimensions of understanding in both these areas—*tefillah* and *berachah*. First, he taught us to instill and reinforce within ourselves the *emunah*, the pure belief, regarding *berachah*, the power that Hashem invested in the uttering of our words, even in the mere formation and vocalization of the sounds. We see the strength of even Esav's belief in *berachos* from how he reacted, from his devastation upon learning that he had lost his father's blessings. Tradition has it that there was an extremely old gentleman living in Vilna to whom the Vilna Gaon had once blurted out in annoyance, *"Lang zolst du leben—May you have a long life."* This is an insignificant remark people say in Yiddish when they are exasperated, and yet, as this story shows, even such a remark can have surprising effects.

It is important that we generate within ourselves the feeling that we are bringing an actual, real benefit to the recipient of our *berachah*; we are doing a true *chesed*.

The Rebbe taught us, and gave us the insight to understand and appreciate, that all this applies to a *berachah* on the physical level of speech. There is, however, no comparison at all to that same *berachah*'s quality and strength when accompanied by positive mental concentration. The fact that the *berachah* has so much power and can accomplish so much just with the "dry words" does not mean that saying it with intent does not play any role or have any effect. On the contrary, a *berachah* said with proper, positive intent has a tremendously awesome effect, many times more than those "dry words" alone—so great, in fact, that the Rebbe compared it to a nuclear explosion.

The greatest revolution the Rebbe brought about in our outlook regarding *berachos* and our appreciation of them, the most magnificent, eye-opening revelation, the most significant insight, was in the area of salutation-oriented *berachos* and blessings. In the course of our normal, everyday life, in conversations, in greetings and salutations, in reactions, exclamations, proclamations, and best wishes for all sorts of occasions, we make statements that are, in actuality, real *berachos*. Our Torah circles are rich in these but so, too, is the contemporary secular culture. It is indeed wonderful to have a multitude of *berachos* as an integral part of our speech, people saying all sorts of niceties and expressing good wishes to one other. The negative side of this is that we grow accustomed to reciting them and their usage is so commonplace that we become callous about regarding them as actual *berachos*. Rather than giving expression to the unique good wishes felt in each person's heart, these greetings and blessings become a mere recitation of formulas. Besides this loss of the uniqueness of people exchanging their intended good wishes, there is not even an awareness that this is a *berachah* being given. All this the Rebbe greatly revolutionized—he opened our eyes to the multitude of *berachos* that we say, and opened our hearts to augment and strengthen them with our sincere thoughts.

This would mean that when wishing a traveler "Have a good trip," one should bear in mind the words of the *berachah*, their implications, and then, in full concentration, itemize the *berachah's* realization: a safe trip and return, as well as success in the endeavors undertaken.

Here are some further examples of good wishes we can concentrate on when we give the most common *berachos*:

"Good morning" — to a Torah learner, we might intend this to mean, have a good learning session, say a good *shiur*. To a businessman, complete some fortuitous deals. To a housewife, the washing machine should do its job and not break down.

"Hearty appetite" — digest the food well and enjoy it.

"*Yasher Koach*" — your strength should increase, to the *gabbai* or whoever has performed a task well.

"*Gezundheit*" — lots of good health to you.

"*Mazel tov*" — good fortune on a million different occasions.

"*Gut Shabbos*" — the *cholent* should be tasty, and may you have a good rest, and may your Shabbos be meaningful.

"*Gut voch*" — Good week; may you suffer no indigestion from the *cholent*.

"*Kol tuv*" — "Live and be well."

"Bon voyage"; "Happy birthday"; "Happy anniversary"; "Have a nice day." And the list goes on.

The reservoirs of the Rebbe's *berachos* were always ready to pour out and consequently to open all the gates Above to shower us with the best of blessings. However, in the framework of walking with the Rebbe I had the opportunity to witness the sun shining in its full glory. Walking with the Rebbe one could observe a firsthand, true to life demonstration of someone who has a sincere desire to bring good, with the understanding of the importance of intent and the sincere belief that it all really works.

I am walking with the Rebbe, and he stops to give a *berachah*. I am standing next to him and I hear his *berachah* clearly and can feel his *kavannah*. There is, however, something very strange taking place, and I am shocked. The Rebbe is giving his *berachah*, and in the place where someone should be standing and receiving it there is … air—empty space. On previous occasions this strange phenomenon *seemed* to be taking place, and I thought that I must be mistaken; but now it is clearly happening.

I cannot deny that I was sort of nervous over this for a while. The Rebbe then explained that he had a tradition from his Rebbe that if one passes the dwelling of an acquaintance and wishes to bestow his best wishes on the friend, he may stop and direct his *berachah* to the friend via his house!

I guess we could call this "airing out" your *berachah*.

Have a nice day.

CHAPTER ELEVEN

It's About Davening

*A*midah—standing, is a term used for the *Shemoneh Esrei* prayer; and walking is seemingly the opposite. So it would seem that *tefillah* does not really have a place in our subject matter—my walks with the Rebbe. In the world of the Rebbe, however, these two came together and met.

Tefillah is one of the cornerstones of our *avodas Hashem*. It is understandable that *davening* played a major role in the Rebbe's life. One could see the Rebbe's high esteem for *tefillah* in his personal *avodah,* and the high priority in which he held it was obvious from the *chinuch* the Rebbe gave us, his *talmidim*. The Rebbe *davened* regularly in a *minyan* with *baalei batim*, nevertheless this did not in any way diminish the quality of his *tefillah*. "Eitzah b'chochmah tachin—With wisdom use practical ingenuity." The Rebbe shared the following with me. The *ba'alei batim*, out of reverence, would wait to start *chazaras hashatz* until the Rebbe had finished *Shemoneh Esrei*. The ba'alei batim themselves would complete *Shemoneh Esrei* very quickly. The Rebbe, whose *davening* took much longer than theirs, felt it was a great imposition to make them wait. We have to understand that during this period of time *baalei batim* would regularly complete their *Shemoneh Esrei* with such exaggerated brevity that it was clearly not an option for the Rebbe to attempt to *daven* at their pace. On the other hand, to make the *baalei batim* wait was, from the Rebbe's point of view, likewise not negotiable. The Rebbe found a unique solution to this dilemma: even though he was still in the middle of his *Shemoneh Esrei*, he would step back three steps as one does upon completing the prayer, thus giving the *baalei batim* their cue to proceed. This left the Rebbe free to soar to his great heights without feeling that he was imposing.

The Rebbe's solution was a radical one: the halachah in the *Shulchan Aruch* (*siman* 104) is very stringent regarding moving from one's place during *Shemoneh Esrei*. According to the *Mishnah Berurah*, if an infant is crying and one finds this disturbing to his concentration, it is permissible to remove oneself from the premises. The same concept could be applied to moving from the spot where one is *davening* because his present location is interfering with his *kavannah*, as in the Rebbe's case, where he was disturbed by knowing he was holding back his congregation from continuing. It is important to take note that for many this would not have been a problem at all. They would not have minded cutting down on the *Shemoneh Esrei* or, contrariwise, to make the *baalei batim* wait would not have been a problem; after all, it is beneficial for them to demonstrate respect for their Rabbi. It is only because the Rebbe took *davening* so seriously, and equally, did not want that *kavod* from the *baalei batim*, that this presented a problem.

In the framework of *vaadim*, which were special groups that met for spiritual training, plus other opportunities, the Rebbe gave tremendously valuable, precious, practical tools with which to improve and upgrade the quality of our *tefillah*. These were in the form of exercises, which, in a down-to-earth and concrete way, slowly led us to solid self-improvement. This chapter is not the proper place to elaborate on all the helpful advice and ideas we received in the *va'adim*, but I would like to presently share some gems. In general our generation suffers from a common difficulty in focusing their concentration properly throughout the entire *Shemoneh Esrei*. The Rebbe's very practical suggestion was to divide the *Shemoneh Esrei* into three parts, and then, in each one of the three *tefillos* of the day, to make an extra effort to concentrate on one of the parts. Since this was more practically realistic and within our reach than trying to concentrate through the entire prayer, it inspired and motivated us to invest special energy.

The most important facet of *Shemoneh Esrei* is generating within oneself the feeling of actually standing before Hashem. R' Chaim Brisker calls this *"cheftzah,"* the defining characteristic of, *Shemoneh Esrei*. This thought must be kept in mind with great consistency, without any lapse. This, too, we find especially difficult in our generation, and here again, the Rebbe's helping hand came to the rescue with a very practical, workable exercise. Whenever we come to the word *"Atah"* in a *berachah*, pause for a moment and think of what the word means, its simple translation—"You," and to Whom we are addressing it. The value of this exercise is much greater than what meets the eye. When done properly, it can generate a feeling of actually standing before Hashem.

There is one *tefillah*-related area in which I feel I gained the most from the Rebbe. He revealed and opened my eyes to the value and appreciation of one of the most important aspects of *tefillah*. The irony in this is that it is an aspect that we are all aware of, and even more amazing, we actually practice. Yet, the Rebbe enlightened us to new dimensions and ramifications of *tefillah*. Let me explain.

The popular perspective on the world of *tefillah* is focused on the three required, structured, daily *Shemoneh Esreis*. The truth, however, is that the power of *tefillah* in its essence is completely independent of, and not at all related or confined to, these *tefillos*. *Tefillah* in essence is not at all connected to any specific time, form, text, or subject. *Tefillah* is coming before Hashem and petitioning a cause, requesting and pleading for some need. It could be for oneself, or for another, or for many. It could be for something vital, pressing, or life-threatening or something non-essential or luxurious. It may be said any time, in any language, and without any special form. It can be repeated as often as one desires. It is important to point out that one may include the Name of Hashem if one chooses, in contrast to formal *berachos* which do not allow any originality on our parts.

The fact that *tefillah* affords unlimited opportunities for appealing for a cause and is not limited to the conventional three-times-a-day *davening* is certainly not a new insight originating with the Rebbe. We find in the *Shulchan Aruch* that when one takes medicine it should be accompanied with a *tefillah* for a *refuah sheleimah*, a speedy recovery. Likewise, the *tefillah* of R' Nechunia ben HaKaneh for daily success in one's Torah study is well known and its recital is widely practiced. The Rebbe, however, opened our eyes to the realization and appreciation of the significant opportunity for a person to be *mispallel* for himself and for the needs of others. One much-overlooked example is the need for a young man or a young woman before going out on a *shidduch* to pray for special Divine guidance. An important point the Rebbe made was that it is appropriate to be *mispallel* for anything a person really wants to acquire. Some people say they would not want to "bother" Hashem for trivial matters, without realizing the implication of that remark. If it is important to you and you really want it, then it is fitting to pray. One example the Rebbe gave was praying for success in a college exam. The person has been studying day and night and has even acquired large "bags" under his eyes. If it was suggested to him to be *mispallel*, he might say: "How can I bother Hashem with my silly exams? I am not even 100 percent sure that Hashem wants me to attend college." All this might be true, but nevertheless, if it is important for you to pass and you are investing so much time and effort studying, how do you expect to do so without Hashem's help? The Rebbe went even further. What about a seemingly meaningless ball game? If it is very important to you and you really care about your side winning, it only makes sense that you should pray.

The Rebbe likewise opened our eyes to new dimensions in being *mispallel* for others. Upon noticing a *Bakshu Rachamim* sign, asking the *tzibbur* to be *mispallel* for someone who is in need of a speedy recovery, the Rebbe suggested saying an immediate *tefillah* for that person. Even people who are concerned simply jot down the name to be mentioned in their regular *Shemoneh Esrei*. The Rebbe pointed out that the opportunity for *chesed* here is infinite. Many of us observe people in need—a typical example would be someone in desperate need of a *shidduch*. A common reaction from onlookers is to throw up their hands, exclaiming that unfortunately they are not *shadchanim*, they know very few people, and therefore they consider themselves completely helpless in this very urgent cause.

Once one understands and practices this mentality of praying for others, the avenues of assistance are opened up—and you are always able to help people with your *tefillos*. One can unfortunately find many situations where there is great need, and there is an opportunity to be of help through *tefillah*.

Our walks afforded a great opportunity to witness the Rebbe putting this lofty ideal into practice.

I am walking with the Rebbe, and the high-pitched wail of an ambulance siren pierces our ears. That is the signal of someone in distress. Even if it is a joyous ride, a healthy young woman on the way to the hospital to deliver a baby, she is still in need of a lot of mercy from Heaven to be blessed with an uneventful, uncomplicated birth and a healthy baby.

In our walk today we pass a hospital. The Rebbe stops, pensively eyeing the building from top to bottom. "Imagine" he says, "a whole building crowded with the sick and suffering. How can we pass without a *tefillah* for them all?"

How can we?

The Rebbe has synthesized walks and prayers.

CHAPTER TWELVE

Frock Coats and Garbage Can Covers

*W*hat it boils down to is, do frock coats mix with garbage can covers?

The scene takes place in the Next World, in the place of retribution: We see a lineup of disreputable characters—gangsters, hoodlums, drug addicts, ruffians, and thieves, awaiting their punishment. Also in the lineup is an individual who does not look as if he belongs there. Not only doesn't he resemble these ruffians, but he looks as if he came straight out of one of the great Kollels. He stands there looking very much out of place, uncomfortable amongst these hoodlums. His name is called out at the roll call and he expresses strong objections. There has been a terrible error, some horrible mix-up. They have this righteous, learned fellow confused with a crook. "No," says the deep, celestial voice, "here there are no mistakes or confusions. Unfortunately, this is exactly where you belong."

"It can't be! I certainly wasn't a criminal, and I had nothing to do with any business dealings or transactions, so how could I have been guilty of any monetary offenses of importance?" The Heavenly Tribunal then, like a bolt of lightning, shocks our pious-looking individual with a presentation of the various, indeed, serious monetary offenses he committed.

For the many who were *zocheh* to be close to the Rebbe, there is a good chance that they will be saved from this scenario. The Rebbe gave us a *poke'ach ivrim chinuch*, training in how to keep our eyes open, to always be aware. And we received special lessons in *Choshen Mishpat*, including revelations regarding a multitude of situations in which there is a prevailing lack of awareness that they are related to *Choshen Mishpat* at all, and consequently that there is any monetary wrongdoing. In most of these situations, the problem is not so much a lack of knowledge of the laws themselves as a lack of realization that these various situations are actually infringements. For this, the Rebbe was magnificent at focusing our attention on the realization that these are in fact wrongdoings.

One area he pointed out to us was the misuse of borrowed items. A classic example was borrowing somebody's pen and indulging in chewing on it, as many people do while lost in thought. Other examples would be borrowing chairs and leaning back on them, thus weakening them and causing them to become prone to breaking more easily; leaning on a store window, as one might do while waiting for a bus; having one's foot protruding in the aisle of a bus or other public place, thereby creating a dangerous obstacle—that carelessly placed foot is sufficient to render one guilty of the specific transgression of creating a hazardous pitfall, even if no one actually trips over it.

An example the Rebbe often gave was that of those who go into a shul, especially one with elderly congregants, and help themselves to a *gemara*, rationalizing that the *gemara* is probably not being used there anyway. The Rebbe used to add that this misappropriated volume might even be *Masechta Bava Kamma*—imagine the farce of a person learning the laws of stealing in *Perek HaGozeil* from a stolen *gemara*. To bring out the point of crystallizing the laws of *Choshen Mishpat* into situations of everyday life the Rebbe used to cite the following story of R' Yisrael Salanter. Once Shabbos the great *tzaddik* was walking with a group of his students on a windy day, all of them wearing high silk hats which contained hard metal bars inside. R' Yisrael cautioned the group to "hold onto your hats," lest the wind blow them into flight and ram them into someone, causing injury. R' Yisrael quoted the *gemara*: "*Avno, sakino, umasa'o sheheniach al rosh hagag v'nafal b'ruach metzuyah*—[One is responsible for damage done by] stones, knives, and sacks placed on the roof and blown off by a normal wind." This is a beautiful example of applying monetary-law concepts from the *gemara* to everyday life.

The examples of general unawareness just cited were brought to our attention by the Rebbe to encourage us to have our antennas up and to be receptive to all manner of similar circumstances. The Rebbe gave us a valuable exercise: to spend a day reviewing our surroundings, searching for previously unrecognized potential sources of violation.

Before plastic came into wide usage, the garbage cans that were placed outside of homes in New York for collection by the Sanitation Department were made of metal and had, likewise, metal covers. In the 1950's a law was passed in New York requiring the covers to be positioned on the cans at all times. Transgressors were penalized with a fine.

I was with the Rebbe, accompanying him on one of our wonderful walks. We were accosted by unusually strong gusts of wind. One such onslaught of wind uprooted a garbage can cover from its respectable place on the can, and it proceeded to roll down the street. As had occurred on other occasions, I suddenly found myself not in the presence of the Rebbe. Where was the Rebbe? The Rebbe, in all his dignified attire and venerable appearance, was off chasing the cover, which he quickly retrieved and returned to its proper place. I questioned whether it was appropriate for the Rebbe to engage in the retrieval of the cover himself. He replied that if he were exempt from this action, the source of his exemption would be the gemara, "*Zaken v'eino l'fi kevodo*—A scholar who encounters the mitzvah of *hashavas aveidah*, returning lost property, in such circumstances that would be beneath his dignity to become involved in, is exempt from the mitzvah." The Rebbe then explained that the criterion for this is how the *chacham* would proceed if it were his own belongings that were lost: would he attempt to retrieve them despite the circumstances being beneath his dignity?

The Rebbe then went on to say, "If it was my garbage can cover rolling down the block, boy would I take off after it!"

CHAPTER THIRTEEN

Enjoy, Enjoy!

*T*n the course of giving a lecture, the Rebbe once requested that every member of the audience should wiggle his toes. He then went on to explain that wiggling the toes is a pleasurable experience because there is a piece of smooth leather at the end of the shoe which is put there especially for the comfort of the wearer. A person could live his entire life never being cognizant of this special comfort. The Rebbe intended to convey something extremely important with this stimulating exercise.

Incidentally, this is a prime example of a teacher extending himself and using ingenuity to capture his audience's attention in a positive way. This is a reflection of the Midrash that relates that R' Akiva once noticed his students dozing while he was giving a *shiur*. He spontaneously posed a question to stimulate them in a positive way: Why was Queen Esther worthy of ruling over 127 provinces? The query accomplished what he had intended and perked up the students. After they had wracked their brains and failed to come up with an answer, R' Akiva surprised them with his solution: Esther had a great ancestor—Sarah Imeinu—who, by virtue of her 127 years of productive life, enabled Esther to become queen over the 127 provinces.

The principle the Rebbe was teaching here is one of the most important in life, affecting both the outlook of our *Yiddishkeit* and our relationship to Hashem. It really is a subject that needs elaboration, and I hope that within our limited framework here we can shed some light on it. We are aware that we must go through a certain amount of discomfort and pain which is ordained for us by Heaven for our personal growth. At the same time we are showered with Heavenly blessings. These are in the form of all kinds of enjoyable experiences. Although we are experiencing countless enjoyable physical sensations, many go by unnoticed, and we are actually completely unaware of them. The Rebbe initiated a revolutionary concept—that we should have our antennas up and we should be sensitive; we must have our awareness buttons turned on and focused. We should attempt to have a conscious attentiveness to these pleasures Hashem has given us. The reasoning behind this is that Hashem *did* create these for our enjoyment and pleasure, and through conscious awareness our pleasure is greatly enhanced. These blessings of pleasure are likewise critical and crucial tendons that connect us to Hashem. By having an appreciation and insight into at least some of the infinite wisdom necessary to produce them, plus the immense gratitude that comes as a direct result of this recognition of the Divine gift, a wholesome, well-founded connection with Hashem is created.

He often quoted the *Kuzari* saying that one of the main reasons we are commanded to recite *berachos* is to focus on and appreciate the object of the *berachah*. This perspective is certainly unique; the conventional thinking is that because we appreciate, we recite the *berachah*, yet according to the *Kuzari*, we recite the *berachah* in order to appreciate. Another great aspect of the Rebbe's elucidation was that we benefit from many of these overlooked pleasures without having to pay for them. As a matter of fact, some of the greatest of pleasures are free of any cost.

Amazing! The generally accepted perspective is that to attain high levels of piety one must avoid, reject, and be cleansed of materialistic pleasures. Often quoted was the *Tosafos* in *Masechta Berachos* that offers an explanation on the *berachah* of *borei nefashos*. The latter part of the text, the *Tosafos* explains, refers to aspects of the creation that were not crucial for man's survival, but rather were created solely for man's pleasure. An example *Tosafos* brings is apples. It is of major importance to consider and to contemplate this statement of *Tosafos*—"Hashem created them solely for man's pleasure." The Rebbe explained that our nourishment process could have been operated exactly along the lines of a car; you pull into a gasoline station and make your request: "fill 'er up." The car receives absolutely no pleasure from the experience. The recharging of a battery likewise is accomplished without the battery experiencing a "high." Hashem could have arranged our sustenance to resemble the medical experience of being nourished intravenously.

Yet Hashem created the enjoyable experience of eating for our pleasure. This opens our eyes to the fact that so much of the creation is for our pleasure: beautiful flowers, beautiful birds, breathtakingly exquisite tropical fish; the world is full of beauty for our enjoyment. Smells, sounds, and sights—the list is almost endless. To do this subject justice really requires an elaboration that is not within the framework of this book. Although the subject is enjoyable and pleasurable (a pun was definitely intended), we can only make a brief reference to it here.

How does this realization affect the relationship of a human to his Creator? How does one feel toward Hashem, Who created such an awesome mechanism for man's enjoyment and pleasure? If one does not have the mindset to focus, to observe, to be aware and appreciate, it will most likely just pass over his head. He will not even be cognizant of its existence, he will not appreciate it, and it surely will not have an effect on his relationship with Hashem. The greatest and most important enlightenment that the Rebbe offered us was the fact that we are actually receiving pleasure constantly, but most often we are completely unaware that the enjoyment is taking place.

Those close to the Rebbe were able to see a clear manifestation of this mentality in him. The Rebbe's favorite and most enjoyable beverage was a glass of water. How much the Rebbe appreciated and admired a garden with beautiful flowers; he so wisely pointed out how blind it is of people to be able to enjoy this floral beauty only when it is the fruit of their own time, effort, and money.

The world of puns itself is a phenomenon which was put into the creation as a form of color in speech. (The art of appreciating colorful vegetation "stems" from training oneself with the proper outlook, not just "flowery speech." One can then see the "rosy" side of life. There is an obligation to "plow" through the "leaves" of correct outlook-building literature, not just "watered-down" articles. This will surely "branch off" to other areas of appreciating the creation. The Rebbe's *sefarim* are very "fertile" sources for this type of mindset. They will help "unearth" the facts, and as a result the person will be well "grounded" in the truth and will then be able to get to the "root" of the matter. He can then with his "two lips" offer true praise to Hashcm.)

The Rebbe pointed out the pleasure of walking past a fruit and vegetable store and feasting our eyes on the wide assortment of treasures available, regardless of whether we intend to buy.

Somewhere, at a certain point in most walks, the Rebbe gave the impression of being about to indulge in something materialistic, something very much out of character for the Rebbe. Taking into account various and numerous considerations, the Rebbe would conclude that the time had arrived for his *"seudas melachim"* of some … fresh … delicious … air! The Rebbe would treat himself to a few inhalations. He would breathe deeply, savoring each breath, and express how wonderful it was. He made sure to let it be known what the bill was, how much it cost. This brings to mind a quote, the words of a perceptive man: "Morning air! If men will not drink of this at the fountainhead of the day, why, then, we must even bottle up some and sell it in the shops for those who have lost their subscription ticket to morning time in this world."

Speaking of profound quotes: "It is perhaps a more fortunate destiny to have a taste for appreciating seashells than to be born a millionaire." The Rebbe, he was surely a millionaire; no, a billionaire, no, a trillion …

CHAPTER FOURTEEN

Yo-Yo's or You-You's?

*F*rom time to time it happened while walking with the Rebbe that he would utter a word here or there that was not clear. It sounded something like "hue" or the letter "u" or maybe just the plain word "you." Finally it became apparent that the word he was repeating was "you," and after a while the picture became even clearer.

Within the framework of paying due respect to someone deserving it, when addressing them, the third person is customarily used. Consequently, the Rebbe was addressed in the third person by his *talmidim*.

Hagaon hakadosh, the leader of his generation, Rabbi Akiva Eiger, had arrived in a certain city where he had been invited to deliver a lecture. The populace turned out in its expected masses to pay tribute and to show their reverence to the *gadol hador*. Picturing this glorious scene, we can see Rabbi Akiva Eiger receiving *kevod melachim*, royal honor. His close students, who were surrounding him, could not help noticing the *gaon* talking to himself, and with a little pressing closer and straining of the ears they were able to hear this great *gaon*, amidst this shower of admiration, whispering derogatory statements about himself. Similarly, this scene has repeated itself time and again with many of our *gedolim* throughout history. These great men were ensuring that they would not be caught in the trap of excessive pride.

When he was already renowned, the Chafetz Chaim once opted to travel alone on a train through Europe. The news of his presence spread through the train. One of the travelers, as did many, set out to find him. As it turned out, the Chafetz Chaim was sitting inconspicuously, wearing his layman's cap as usual, incognito, in the corner of one of the cars. This cap itself has a special significance to our subject. Here we find one of the greatest sages of the generation and an outstanding leader donning a cap generally worn by a simple layman. Recently I happened to come across a photo of the famous sage and *dayan* of the city of Brisk, HaRav Simchah Zelig, and he likewise was wearing this layman's cap. This is a prime example of the humble demeanor of our great ones. Returning to our train journey, our traveler, very excited and pumped with adrenalin in anticipation of seeing the Chafetz Chaim, was not aware that the elderly man he was approaching was R' Yisrael Meir of Radin himself. He asked with excitement if this gentleman knew of the whereabouts of the Chafetz Chaim. The Chafetz Chaim told the man to calm down and that there was no need to be so excited. The man, a little annoyed, replied that he could not wait "to see the man of such virtue." The Chafetz Chaim again suggested that the man calm down and that the Chafetz Chaim was not so great. This, the man felt, was taking things too far, and with that he wound up and landed a firm smack on the cheek of the Chafetz Chaim! The Chafetz Chaim's acting this way and saying what he did was, of course, in the light of this "running from *kavod*" mentality. We have a tradition that our outward actions have a strong influence on our innermost faculties, and therefore the outward actions are often used as a tool to access the innermost ones. However, in these instances of running from *kavod*, our Sages were doing it out of true feelings of humility.

Our *chachamim*, in their quest for truth and honesty, did not satisfy themselves by just adopting the outward behavior of running from honor. They scrutinized this behavior under the clear magnifiers of their spiritual microscopes. The *Mesillas Yesharim* explains that there is a type of running from *kavod* and acting in a manner indicating humility that in actuality is a distinct form of *kavod*-seeking. A person like this poses as one running from *kavod* for the purpose of gaining *kavod* as a supposedly humble being.

It was very clear to all who were close with the Rebbe that he was a living example of one who escapes from being the recipient of honor, and that this behavior was certainly meant in all sincerity. Although the incident I related in this chapter is not necessarily walk-related, my memories of this experience are somehow always connected with the walks. As it turned out, what this "you" was all about was that when the Rebbe would hear himself addressed in the third person, he would show his disapproval by giving directives to be addressed as "you"—as if he were an ordinary layman!

CHAPTER FIFTEEN

"Body" Guard

"Now is not the time to hear your *chiddush*."

"Now is not the time for me to answer your question."

"Now is not the time for Torah."

"Now is not the time to think of any *avodas Hashem*."

"Now is not the time even to think of Hashem."

What could the Rebbe have been referring to when he made these statements?

Included among the areas in which the Rebbe gave us *chizuk* was the importance of personal body care. It was a little unusual to hear the Rebbe speak about this, considering his role as a spiritual guide. He impressed upon us the importance of dental care: taking regular care of our oral hygiene, going very regularly for dental checkups, making sure to select a good dentist. The Rebbe explained that with poor teeth a person cannot chew his food well and consequently, he will not digest his food properly (the digestive system begins with chewing), and this may lead to serious stomach disorders that can eventually wreak havoc to the whole body.

The Rebbe emphasized the importance of taking good care of one's eyes. This includes periodic eye examinations and great caution in refraining from anything that could cause harm to one's eyesight. This is applicable to any human being, but especially to one who is seriously committed to the service of Hashem. As for a *ben Torah*, how supreme and vital his eyesight is for his Torah learning.

The Rebbe spoke of the importance of eating properly and getting the requisite amount of sleep and rest.

The Rebbe often quoted *Chazal* relating the episode in which Hillel excused himself from the presence of his students on the premise that he had a guest at home to whom he had to attend. The students, knowing that there was no guest at his home, pressed for an explanation. Hillel explained that he was referring to the body and soul relationship, and that caring for his body's nourishment was tantamount to preoccupation with the needs of a guest.

The Rebbe also gave a tremendous insight into the high priority of the requirement that one do *chesed* for himself. The closer the relative, the greater the requirement to do acts of kindness. If both an individual's father and uncle are drowning and he can save only one person, he is obligated to save his father. The flip side of this would naturally be the closer the relative, the greater the sin if one causes him harm or distress. One's closest "relative" is himself, which explains why suicide is considered such a grave sin. All this gives us a perspective on the responsibility one has for the care of his person.

With regard to awareness of personal body care, the walks with the Rebbe, our theme throughout these chapters, are themselves one of the greatest indications of his conscientiousness in this matter. The Rebbe's walks were motivated purely for this purpose. To quote an apt saying: "Walking is the exercise that needs no gym. It is a prescription without medicine; weight control without diet; a cosmetic found in no drugstore. It is a tranquilizer with no pill; therapy with no psychoanalyst; a fountain of youth that is no legend. A walk is a vacation that does not cost a cent." Fresh new reports come out constantly in the popular health field, applauding, praising, and recommending walking as the solution for countless ailments and as constructive advice for general well-being.

A group of us is walking with the Rebbe, deeply immersed in a Torah discussion which is suddenly interrupted by the Rebbe. "Now, at the corner, full attention must be given only to the business of crossing the street. One must look in all directions and give this his undivided concentration. Remember to look out for bicycles—they come swiftly and quietly and can do a lot of damage, *chas v'shalom*. This is no time for Torah, no time for *chizuk*, no time even for thinking of Hashem—just one for the road ..."

CHAPTER SIXTEEN

Short and Wet

I can still feel the wetness of my soaked clothing in my memory of walking in the rain with the Rebbe, this time without any protection from the storming torrents. The following is the story behind this wet walk. Generally speaking, in the early years at the Rebbe's shul, the Young Israel of Rugby, there was no *minyan* for Minchah and Maariv. The *baalei batim* were young men who were committed to their jobs and were not home by sunset. However, there was a brief period during the summer when sunset was at its latest, and that enabled the *baalei batim* to be present for these prayers. On one of these bright summer evenings, there was a sudden change in the weather. Dark clouds, sailing in, covered the sun and then the darkness broke into a violent thunderstorm. Nobody present was prepared for the sudden deluge. *Davening* was over, and the whole congregation, including the Rebbe, were faced with going out and braving the showers. Everyone sighed with relief when a hero appeared on the scene handing the Rebbe an umbrella; he had obviously rushed home and back to fetch protection for the revered Rabbi. To our amazement, the Rebbe thanked the "do-gooder" profusely but refused to accept the proffered umbrella. The Rebbe explained to me on our wet walk home that when everyone is forced to brave a storm, and one single individual has the "luck" of obtaining "salvation" before the eyes of them all, you can be sure that he will not have any *hatzlachah* from it.

This important principle that the Rebbe taught us is diametrically opposite to the outlook and mentality of our present-day culture. People feel a need to show off their precious possessions, causing themselves awesome losses. If they understood this in the proper light they would hide their acquisitions in a most modest manner instead of showing off. When moving into a new home, people cannot wait to give a guided tour to their guests—it almost seems as if this were the purpose of it all. If we only understood the damage we might be bringing on ourselves, we would make polite excuses instead, and avoid this behavior like we would the plague.

So there we were, soaked through from the rain, but better that than suffer the repercussions of being the only ones with the umbrella.

CHAPTER SEVENTEEN

"The Saddest Day"

alks are always conducive to sharing stories, and I was *zocheh* to hear quite a few personal tales from the Rebbe in the course of our walks together. I wish to share the following story because of its importance in the Rebbe's life and what we can learn from it. The Rebbe called it "the saddest day" of his life.

The great *gaon* and *tzaddik*, R' Isaac Sher *zt"l*, the *rosh yeshivah* of the renowned Slabodka Yeshivah, came from Europe to the U.S. to raise money for this notable Torah center. While in New York, he used the opportunity of his visit to America to deliver several speeches. One of these "lectures" was attended by a young potential star—the Rebbe. The chemistry between them was at its best and it ignited a burning desire in the Rebbe to follow R' Isaac Sher back to Slabodka and become a new *talmid*, ready to open his heart and mind to a whole new *derech*. This entailed making a complete overhaul on his purpose and direction in life. A most magnificent and significant *hashgachah* led up to all this, as told in the following story.

The Rebbe related that he was in his hometown of Baltimore in the office of the principal of a yeshivah, waiting to be interviewed. The Rebbe had gone down south after earning his teaching credentials in a New York yeshivah. The Rebbe related how he had learned in this very yeshivah as a child, and his life ambition had been to educate himself and achieve the proper credentials so that he could some day return and serve as an educator there himself. This ambition was no small matter; it meant leaving home for years and facing the physical hardships of learning in an out-of-town yeshivah. All this, in addition to the great mental effort and conscientiousness necessary to maintain a high scholastic record. As we picture the Rebbe seated in the yeshivah office, waiting for his interview, we are focusing on the climax of years of yearning, followed by years of diligent studies and self-sacrifice. The Rebbe felt confident about getting the position. The person in charge of hiring was well aware and appreciative of the Rebbe's background story; he knew that he was a successful past student of the yeshivah who had always aspired to teach there.

Waiting with the Rebbe was another young man, a schoolmate from the same New York yeshivah, also applying for the same position. The Rebbe did not feel in the least pressured or threatened by his competition. This young man was a complete stranger here, whereas this was the Rebbe's alma mater. Also, the Rebbe had taken his studies in New York very seriously, even going beyond the usual yeshivah schedule and using his free time to advance his Torah knowledge. (This was how the Rebbe had gained his unusually broad knowledge of *Tanach*.) The other fellow had used his free time at yeshivah to indulge in sports activities. The Rebbe felt, as the saying goes, that he really had it in the bag, and with good reason. Who can imagine, then, the great disappointment and heartache the Rebbe felt when, at the climax of so much time and energy invested for this teaching position, it was given to his ball-playing colleague.

This was indeed "the saddest day" of the Rebbe's life.

The Rebbe, feeling broken, eventually left Baltimore, as remaining there would be empty and purposeless. He made his way aimlessly back to New York. Following this terrible disappointment, the Rebbe had his historical meeting with R' Isaac Sher. The Rebbe had a degree and teaching credentials; he was ready to go on with life, with his career. By the standards of the day, he was an accomplished individual. Yet, what could the world have gained from the elementary-school teacher the Rebbe might have become at that point? But through this most unpleasant experience the Rebbe was blessed by Heaven with circumstances that changed his whole life and put him on the path that led to his evolving into the giant that we eventually knew. Going to learn in Europe in the famed Slabodka Yeshivah opened new horizons—the Slabodka approach to *Tanach*; the world of studying the greatness of man; entering the orbit of *Chovos HaLevavos*, particularly *Shaar HaBechinah*, for which he became especially famous; and above all, it offered the Rebbe an opportunity to sit and learn undisturbed and excel in his knowledge of *Shas* and Torah in general. After years of learning in Slabodka it was time for him to marry. He was deemed worthy for the daughter of Rav Lessin, a great *talmid chacham*, a *baal mussar*, and the Rav of Neishtadt. The Rebbe was of such high caliber that he, too, was worthy of being the Rav in that city. It was actually included in the marriage contract that the Rebbe would take over the position after his father-in-law. But World War II and the Holocaust interfered with this plan. The Rebbe eventually returned to the U.S., a shining star, ready to take on America.

So this, the Rebbe's saddest day, turned out to be his luckiest. Hashem is always looking out for us, and nothing can ever happen to us that is not for our absolute benefit. This is a subject the Rebbe spoke about often. He would quote *Chovos HaLevavos*, which states this principle and explains that when we do experience something that appears not to be good, with some thought and delving into the matter we can often discover its true benefit. Sometimes the truth of what we have to gain from the experience cannot be seen or understood until some time later, even many years. There are also experiences whose benefits we will never understand in the course of our lifetime, and we will only get the true insight into them in the next world. *Chovos HaLevavos* gives a startling example for this idea which the Rebbe cited many times:

Our scene opens on a wayfarer traveling by foot on a dusty road of old. It is midday; the sun is beating down at its strongest. Our traveler is forced to take a break. He chooses the shade of an old wall at the side of the road. There he stretches out to take a snooze and in no time falls into a deep sleep, alongside many other travelers doing the same. His peaceful rest is abruptly interrupted by the sensation of a warm, putrid liquid pouring onto him, "courtesy" of a dog. He has no choice but to rise and continue on his way, hoping the sun will dry him as quickly as possible. Whenever this fellow recalls that experience, it of course evokes a very unhappy, negative memory. What he does not know, and probably will never find out, is that after his unscheduled departure the old wall that was shading him suddenly collapsed, and all those seemingly lucky travelers who had continued their slumber dry and undisturbed were crushed to death by the falling stones! And so our wayfarer goes on with his life, enveloped in this sad memory.

I am sure the Rebbe is forever basking in the joy and happiness of that day in Baltimore, his saddest day.

CHAPTER EIGHTEEN

"The Happiest Day"

I wish to share another story the Rebbe related to me within the framework of our walks. He referred to it as the "happiest day of his life."

As mentioned in the previous chapter, the Rebbe left home and his native city of Baltimore to attend a yeshivah in New York. Needless to say, this endeavor called for an inordinate amount of self-sacrifice. Daily life in yeshivah in those days was difficult. The Rebbe took his studies very seriously, which required yet a higher level of commitment. And the Rebbe demanded even more of himself by making use of his "free time" to further his studies in order to become knowledgeable in *Tanach*.

The following is an illustration of how seriously the Rebbe was involved in his learning: At that period of history, the illustrious R' Yaakov Yosef Herman was the lighthouse of Torah and the fortress of

Torah-true ideals. He was the great personality described in the book "All for The Boss" written by his daughter, the famous Rebbetzin Ruchoma Shain. Long before that book was written, the Rebbe proclaimed publicly many times that a book should be written about Rav Herman. Rebbetzin Shain told me that in fact the Rebbe's prodding was one of her main motivations for eventually writing her father's story. Rav Herman lived near the yeshivah that the Rebbe was attending. He had the wisdom and insight to realize that many students in the yeshivah were in dire need of spiritual reinforcement which they were not receiving under the auspices of the yeshivah. Rav Herman, therefore, took it upon himself to provide an unofficial *shiur* in *Mesillas Yesharim*. Where would these private *chizuk* sessions be given? It was the Rebbe who hosted them in his dormitory room. This included responsibility for the tedious task of rounding up chairs for the many participants. Also included was helping Rav Herman to climb up to the dormitory room via the window!

The yeshivah itself that Rebbe was attending had world-renowned scholars delivering *shiurim* at that time. Putting this whole picture together, an image is produced of the Rebbe as a very serious Torah student. Imagine my surprise and shock, then, when the Rebbe made the following statement to me: "The happiest day of my life was while I was attending the yeshivah in New York; it was the day they informed me that I had achieved a high enough status that I was no longer required to attend a *gemara shiur*."

One's initial reaction upon hearing that someone who had such a great thirst for Torah knowledge, and was so serious and devoted, and yet had such a distaste for a *gemara shiur* that being released from the requirement to attend produced such great happiness, is surely one of shock.

However, the fact that the Rebbe excelled in his studies, despite his displeasure, obvious dissatisfaction, and inner rejection of the *shiurim* casts even more light on the extent of the Rebbe's self-sacrifice and personal investment during the course of his years in the yeshivah.

There is an aspect of all this that is extremely, awesomely, significant and brings with it significant ramifications in our own lives, to our families and the people in our circle of acquaintances. This surprising but simple episode reveals one of the burning, pressing issues of our day. One has tried so many *shiurim* and does not find his place in any of them. What is his self-image regarding his study of Torah? Is he left with the feeling that he is not really cut out for studying Torah, that Torah learning is not for him, that he must relinquish any plans for Torah study or growth and withdraw from his present affiliation to any kind of learning institution or program? Likewise, we observe friends or acquaintances in the same predicament—with a score of zero when it comes to appreciating a *shiur*. What about our students? How do we deal with a child that rejects *shiurim*? "Simply not cut out for Torah"?

Here the Rebbe created for us a nuclear explosion. The Rebbe had such a great interest in learning, had such a burning ambition, had such clearly defined goals set out for himself, with such sincerity, and yet at the same time had such an extreme aversion to attending a *gemara shiur* from the great masters, that the release from the requirement to attend was the cause of his supreme happiness. This is so vital, so basic, so inspiring for all those plagued with this very problematic, devastating *shiur*-allergy syndrome. Rebbe's example is a powerful lesson—not to allow a resistance to *shiurim* to reflect in any way on the evaluation of a person's capacity and abilities for Torah learning and growth, whether one is evaluating himself, his child, or his student. The lesson is very simple, clear and blazing: not everyone is cut out for *shiurim*. Desire for *shiurim* and success in them has no connection with ability or potential to reach even the highest levels of Torah growth.

It is of utmost importance to bear in mind that the popular or conventional *shiurim* and systems of *chinuch* in general are not designed for everyone. There are people ranging from fine, average scholars to exceptionally brilliant geniuses who were shipwrecked in life by the educational system, simply because the chemistry was not right for their personality type. Recently, in a conversation I had with the principal of one of the most prominent *chadarim* in our city, he informed me that in the existing educational system there is an expectation of success from one-third of the class. One-third of the class is not expected to keep up at all, and the middle third floats in a gray area. So many bright young children, who seem to be headed for such success, experience a complete downfall soon after they enter the educational system.

The great *gaon* and *tzaddik*, the Steipler Rav *zt"l*, the Torah leader of *Klal Yisrael* in the past generation, was having difficulty with his son Chaim. Little Chaim was putting up resistance to his Torah studies. The Steipler, out of desperation, resorted to implementing strict disciplinary measures, but without success. The Steipler presented this serious problem to his brother-in-law, the famed Chazon Ish. His seemingly radical advice was that Chaim should immediately stop being taught with the usual approach and system used in the yeshivos. No deep analysis, not any analysis; no early *Rishonim*, no late *Rishonim*, no *Acharonim*, not even any *Tosafos*—just plain *gemara* and *Rashi* straight through until the end of the *masechta*. After this, on to the next *masechta* and then the next, until the completion of *Shas*. Eventually, this was repeated with the addition of *Tosafos* and then other *Rishonim*. The obvious point here is the Chazon Ish's open-mindedness and readiness to be flexible enough to think of the unconventional advice that produced this *gadol*, R' Chaim Kanievsky *shlita*—one of the great leaders of our generation. The Rebbe, in the example of his own life, and likewise, the *gedolim* have demonstrated for us the sensitivity and flexibility necessary for training ourselves, our children, and our students. I hope that this account of the Rebbe's happiest day will bring loads of happiness to many in *Klal Yisrael*.

CHAPTER NINETEEN

Pitch vs. Pitch

oday one of Rebbe's *baalei batim* is joining us on our walk. There is something very special about this man; he is one of Rebbe's personal prodigies. When Rebbe began working in Young Israel of Rugby, it was a Young Israel branch whose members were at the lowest spiritual and social levels. Rebbe was successful in raising its members to top-level, outstanding, model *baalei batim*.

Rebbe's efforts had taken root, and this young man already had a young son enrolled in a top yeshivah elementary school. He had a matter of *chinuch* to discuss with the Rebbe. The subject in question pertained to his son's free time. Should this time be occupied by giving him music lessons or should the time be spent just playing ball? Anyone hearing the question would quickly reply that both are positive recreation, and if the child enjoys learning music, both are enjoyable pastimes. However, when finished playing ball, the child has nothing to show, whereas if his spare time is used to learn an instrument, the child is left with practical knowledge that can come to use in many different ways in the future.

The Rebbe's advice was that since the goal was that the child should grow to be a *talmid chacham*, the ball playing was sufficient to supply a relaxing pastime. Even though this activity appears to be a relative waste of time, the possibilities of complicated side effects are minimal. In contrast, learning an instrument brings a concrete danger of creating an interest on the child's part in furthering himself in the field. This can deter his inspiration, interest, and growth in developing into a *ben Torah*.

We can appreciate the quality of this *baal habayis* (and the Rebbe's handiwork) from the fact that he had the sensitivity and the awareness to realize the importance of asking such a question. Also to be greatly admired is the Rebbe's keen insight into the proper *chinuch* guidance.

This is just an example of one of the multiple guidelines and principles that are an absolute necessity in *chinuch*.

There is a lack of insight presently in the field of *chinuch*, especially regarding raising our children. Perhaps this was a special wisdom that was passed down from one generation to the next, from fathers and mothers to sons and daughters, something that does not happen today. A wisdom lost? The Divine plan has provided us with an opportunity to continue to access this wisdom. A number of outstanding *talmidei chachamim*, wise advisers, and religious professional counselors have authored outstanding books on the subject, full of wisdom. This is something which until recently was not available. Anything that was written on the subject was authored by irreligious people and full of anti-Torah ideas.

Because of the extreme importance of this matter, I wish to share the following list of reading material on the subject. The names listed just happen to be known to me and are not by any means based on selective research. I am sure that there must be other good material that does not appear on this list.

- *My Child, My Disciple* by Rabbi Noach Orlowek
- *Successful Chinuch* by Rabbi Wagschal
- *Make Me, Don't Break Me* by Rabbi Moshe Gans
- *Raising Children to Care* by Miriam Adahan
- *Effective Jewish Parenting* by Miriam Levi
- *Woman to Woman* (the chapter on *chinuch*) by Rebbetzin Esther Greenberg
- *Criticizing Children* by Rabbi Avi Shulman
- *Educating our Children* by Rabbi Hillel Brisk
- *The Eternal Jewish Home* by Rabbi Yoel Schwartz
- *Partners With Hashem* by Rabbi Meir Wikler
- *Chinuch in Turbulent Times* by Rabbi Dov Brezak

There are likewise many audio-cassettes by outstanding authorities, including "Realizing Your Parenting Potential" by Rabbi Yakov Horowitz.

Since this kind of material is the main source for the wisdom of *chinuch* today, the extreme importance and necessity of going through the books is quite evident. No one would ever consider using an expensive, complicated, delicate electronic appliance—that can be ruined as a result of misuse—without first reading the instruction manual. It is incomparably worse to tamper with the *chinuch* of a child, ignorantly pushing buttons and levers that consequently cause havoc and devastation. I unfortunately have come into contact with many victims of these tragedies. Very often the parents are quoted as saying, "We learned from the mistakes we made with our older children" (as told over to me by the unfortunate "older children").

One of most vital rules of *chinuch* is to establish and always maintain a warm relationship with the one we are guiding. A most striking demonstration of this was evident in the life of the *gadol hador* of the last generation, the Steipler, who was known for the time he spent developing a warm and close relationship with his children and grandchildren. To really appreciate this it is important to bear in mind the Steipler's phenomenal *hasmadah*. So great was the Steipler's diligence that once, on his way to the *beis midrash*, he overheard two students discussing a problem of *shatnez* commonly found in certain jackets. Not wishing to take any time from his studies to investigate the matter, the *gaon* ripped out the lining of his jacket and immediately resumed learning.

The Rebbe, who was extremely careful how he spent every minute, went out of his way to demonstrate his warmth and establish a connection with his grandchildren and great-grandchildren. He himself went to toy stores and kept a stock of personally selected toys that he presented to the children. A young man, the son of one of the Rebbe's close students, recently related to me that one of his early childhood memories of the Rebbe is being presented with a toy by him.

So we are catching the ball, not the tune. Here's the pitch—and it's a grand slam homerun.

CHAPTER TWENTY

The Peak of
Mount Everest

*O*ur scene opens in some pretty meadowland on the outskirts of a Lithuanian village. The trickle of the flowing waters of the brook is intermingled with the chirping of multitudes of wild birds and the rustling of the brush in the winds. Besides the breathtaking beauty of the scene there is nothing unusual, except for one very strange sight. In the middle of the field we find the Rebbe seated on the grass, staring at a flower with an abstracted expression on his face—in fact, an expression that might be more accurately described as "spaced-out."

On one of our walks the Rebbe shared what he called "the highest spiritual experience he had had in his life." He described how, when he was learning in Slabodka Yeshivah, during the summer break, he occasionally hiked in the Lithuanian hills and fields, indulging in the joy of coming close to Hashem's creation in its natural state. On one of these excursions he sat and stared at a flower, analyzing its components, appreciating its beauty, and basking in the brilliant warmth of Hashem's infinite wisdom. The Rebbe explained to me that he sat, preoccupied this way, for an hour. When he was finished, he had an awesome feeling of closeness with Hashem and saw the Divine hand in creation with an outstanding clarity. He then added that this was to such an extent that it actually came close to *nevuah* (prophecy). This contemplation, the Rebbe said, produced the greatest spiritual experience he had ever had in his life and led him to supreme heights.

Amazing—absolutely amazing; amazing that it happened, and amazing that the Rebbe repeated it to me.

Now we are all inspired, and yearn to have the same experience. No problem, just sit down on the grass somewhere and stare at a flower for an hour. Of course, this undoubtedly will not propel us to the supreme heights reached by the Rebbe. What is missing?

When the Rebbe verbalized his experience of staring at the flower he described his absolute, consistent, unbroken concentration. Consistent, constant, unbroken thought—let us delve into this. There are those of us who merited to receive guidance and training from the Rebbe in acquiring various spiritually commendable traits. We met once a week and he assigned mental exercises for us to do. These covered a wide range of aspects of *avodas Hashem*, from all kinds of matters pertaining to Hashem Himself, to matters pertaining to one's fellow man. These included true appreciation for the various parts of the body, food, and clothing. We also had "exercises" to learn to appreciate different individuals. There was one common denominator in *"uvdos"* (exercises), as the Rebbe called them, and that was that most of them were mental exercises, taking from 1 to 3 minutes. When one heard what the *uvda* could accomplish and what its duration was, the usual reaction was, "Just for 3 minutes? I'll do it for 15 minutes or half an hour— or an hour!" The secret was that it had to be *intensive and uninterrupted thought*. "No problem?" Just try it for 1 minute and see how difficult it really is.

Somehow these ingredients—intensive and uninterrupted thought—are keys or catalytic agents that make their way to the depth of the heart, and implant a minute, yet concrete ability to control the desired trait.

The *Mesillas Yesharim*, in Chapter 26, deals with the trait of *kedushah*, the highest level a person can reach making use of his own efforts. Consistent with the system the Ramchal prescribes for acquiring traits, he suggests connecting oneself in thought with Hashem. This appears to be something quite simple in proportion to the loftiness of the trait. Again, the answer and the secret lie in the intensity and consistency of the thought.

The *Baal HaTanya*, in Chapter 3, explains that if a person does not harness his mental powers to implant within himself the realization of the presence of Hashem intensively and consistently, the *neshamah* will not produce true fear and love of Hashem, but rather, false, imaginary fantasies.

One minute of pure, focused thought can eventually bring a person to the greatest heights. It is unimaginable to what sphere an hour's concentrated, uninterrupted thought can elevate a person. The Rebbe broke the record for reaching the highest summit.

CHAPTER TWENTY-ONE

Sincerely, Hashem

*I*magine walking through the streets of Yerushalayim in the times of the *Beis HaMikdash*. One can actually feel the holiness. As for cleanliness, the streets are immaculate; when it comes to modesty, the women dress inconspicuously. There is a tangible feeling of awe and fear of Heaven; as *Chazal* explain the words, *"Ki miTzion teitzei Torah"*—by observing the awe and the fear of Heaven displayed by the *Kohanim*, one is inspired to make a strong commitment to Torah study. As one wanders down the street and eavesdrops on the clusters of people engaged in conversation, all he picks up is a broad range of Torah discussions. The general atmosphere is one of joy. This is something that is emphasized strongly, and this emphasis can be seen by the fact that there are virtually no business dealings, since there is generally nervous tension involved in sales transactions. Thus there is an interesting mixture of seriousness, awe, and joy in the air.

What is this I see? A commotion and a crowd headed this way. What can this be? A bride, a groom? It doesn't seem so. The dedication of a Torah scroll? Not this either. Maybe it is a *pidyon peter chamor* parade and they are escorting and dancing around the donkey? I can't say that it is this either. The huge crowd is getting closer and I must say there is really quite a commotion. I now position myself so that I can view the center of the activity, and what I can see is a young woman looking terrified, surrounded by an antagonistic-looking crowd. This is my first exposure to this kind of experience, and I certainly hope it is the last. A *sotah*: a married woman who is seriously suspected of being unfaithful to her husband. What a heartbreaking, tragic sight!

But why did *I* have to be a witness to this? *Chazal* explain that the *parshiyos* of "*nazir*" and "*sotah*" were placed in close proximity in order to transmit the lesson that if one unfortunately witnesses a *sotah*, he should abstain from wine, since that beverage is conducive to immodest behavior. This drink causes a breakdown of our defenses, leaving us much less likely to take the necessary precautions to keep ourselves away from the trap of promiscuity.

The Rebbe pointed out that *Chazal* stress that one who is *witness* to the *sotah* should take the precautionary measure of not consuming wine. Merely being confronted with the phenomenon of a *sotah* and the obvious dangers of laxness should be a sufficient cause of alarm to make us decide to take special precautions. There is a very important principle here, perhaps one of the most important in the whole Torah framework. The giving of the Torah on Sinai was the most open, major communication Hashem ever made to the world in general and to *Klal Yisrael* in particular. This was the enlightenment Hashem gave the world, revealing His will.

The Rebbe went on to explain that this was the major, awesome communication, but Hashem continues perpetually to communicate with the world, with individual nations, and with each and every human, as an ongoing process. This is accomplished primarily through *hashgachah pratis*—the Divine hand managing and controlling everything in the universe. Through the nature of the events that confront us, Hashem reveals what He wishes to transmit. Rav Aharon Kotler *zt"l* was upset when suddenly an immodestly dressed woman appeared before him. When questioned as to why he felt such anguish despite his complete innocence, he explained that what disturbed him was the significance of the Divine message directed at him through the incident that had occurred. Needless to say, one must have keen insight and understanding in order to know how to interpret a Divine "message."

This is a subject about which I heard the Rebbe speak many times, and it was this topic the Rebbe selected to expound upon on our walk one particular morning. To illustrate his theme, the Rebbe revealed to me an important missing link from his life story. After returning from Slabodka in Europe, the Rebbe was appointed to a position in Chelsea, Massachusetts. But how did he make the transition from Chelsea to Yeshivas Chaim Berlin?

Rebbe explained to me on a number of occasions that when he arrived in Chelsea, he found it void of Torah observance. However, it had once been a thriving Torah center. There had been *batei midrashim* on almost every street, many occupied by groups of very learned laymen. Among these were groups that were well-versed in the entire *Shas*. It was during this golden era that the glorious title, "the Vilna of America," was bestowed upon this city. This brings to light a relatively unknown phenomenon. Present-day America is filled with a multitude of cities void of Torah and its observance. When visiting these locations, one assumes that he is treading upon ground never before touched by an observant Jew. The truth, however, is that many of these were once glorious, thriving religious communities. I myself once had occasion to be in Augusta, Georgia. It was completely devoid of any sign of anything Jewish. I had the strange feeling that I was the first Jew to tread upon this soil. As it turned out, the very area I was visiting had once been a center of intensive Torah activity, with *batei midrashim*, *batei knessios*, and *mikvaos*—in Augusta, Georgia!

The United States was once studded with these Torah-filled cities, learned Torah scholars, and knowledgeable laymen. What happened is a spiritual holocaust. The fact that there was such a large-scale spiritual catastrophe in the United States is relatively unknown. It would be extremely valuable to have an insight into the exact cause of this massive spiritual breakdown. I suspect it was a lack of insight and clarity on the part of the older generation as to the nature of the differing mentality and way of life in this New World of America, and the challenges it posed. R' Yaakov Yosef Herman (the hero of *All for the Boss*) was one of the few who had this clear vision and an understanding of how to deal with the situation. I would like, at this point, to pay a modest tribute to my own great-grandparents and grandparents, who were also among this minority of heroes who exhibited the insight and strength to withstand the spiritual turbulence of the times.

The Rebbe now found himself planted in this spiritual desert of a community. One of his first moves was to establish a survival unit for himself by arranging to take over a *gemara* class for laymen. He managed to do this by actually buying the right to teach the group— for the price of $100, which at that time was an enormous sum of money. The Rebbe was eventually successful in establishing a thriving yeshivah, from which many boys went on to study in the major yeshivos of New York. The success of his yeshivah is relatively unknown. Chelsea was so far from Torah and any aspirations toward it that when the Rebbe first announced his plan to open a yeshivah, he was met with unanimous opposition, even from the so-called religious townspeople. The spirit of pessimism was so strong that eventually there was a public demonstration against the Rebbe and his idea of establishing a yeshivah. On one occasion the Rebbe showed me an old, yellowed clipping: it was a news item describing this mass demonstration against him.

The rest, however, is history—a success story of how the Rebbe persisted and the yeshivah took hold and flourished. Now came the missing link—the revelation of how the Rebbe's transition came about, from Rabbi in Chelsea to *mashgiach* in Chaim Berlin. A crisis developed when the educational needs of the Rebbe's own children could no longer be filled in Chelsea and it became absolutely crucial for them to be transplanted to a strong Torah community. The Rebbe was faced with the extremely pressing dilemma of where, and how, to go. He was indeed very much perplexed. At this point the telephone rang, and, as the Rebbe related, on the other end was a voice that said the following: "This is Yitzchak Hutner. Would you accept the position of *mashgiach* in my yeshivah?" Without the slightest hesitation, a positive response was given. The Rebbe pointed out to me that this crucial, critical episode took a mere few seconds. The Rebbe gracefully ejected himself out of Chelsea and landed securely, appropriately, at Yeshivas Chaim Berlin in Brooklyn. (The yeshivah in Chelsea successfully continued under the leadership of one of the Rebbe's prize *talmidim*.)

After relating all of the above, the Rebbe explained that the main point and outstanding moral of these events was the *hashgachah pratis*, the constant watch, care, and control that Hashem demonstrated. The principle of Divine supervision is one of our most basic tenets. But more significant than an intellectual adherence to this belief is the realization and perception of it in our lives: a tremendously profound concept—the understanding that Hashem, the King and Creator of the entire universe, is watching over us, caring and showing His concern with in-depth supervision of even the most minute of details, maneuvering our affairs and endeavors for our utmost benefit.

The next step of this concept is the most mind-boggling of all. Through His control over our destiny, the events of our lives, and the things we experience, Hashem is actually communicating with us in a very personal way.

As the Rebbe explained, the Divine wisdom has arranged for an individual a rendezvous with a *sotah* and her entourage. This is a "message" from Hashem, a "diagnosis" that he has a spiritual deficiency and a weakness toward women; he must take the necessary precaution of refraining from wine.

And so, we, too, continuously receive our Divine communications, signed, "Sincerely yours, Hashem."

CHAPTER TWENTY-TWO

Down Willie's Hatch

O n one memorable walk the Rebbe shared the following: The opening scene takes place at the famous Slabodka Yeshivah. We are surprised to see a shocked look on the Rebbe's face. He has run into an acquaintance and is completely taken aback to see him here.

This story begins in the New York yeshivah where the Rebbe had learned some years earlier. Unfortunately, there were students there who did not take their studies, or for that matter anything else, seriously. There was one young man there that we could say was most outstanding in his laxity and lack of ambition.

Actually, only a small minority of students took their studies seriously at that period of time. Among these, there was a tiny fraction who were so moved as to aspire to continue their Torah studies. Among this small number, there were a few very special individuals who had the fire of Torah burning so brightly in their hearts that they were willing to make the tremendous personal investment and self-sacrifice of traveling to Europe to intensify their Torah study. These few dedicated individuals lifted themselves above the various allurements that America presented to her youth at that time, especially the pursuit of a career. They represented a very high level of idealism. In Europe there were numerous yeshivos. The yeshivah of Slabodka was outstanding for both its excellent scholastic level and for inspiring the students to perfection in character training and *yiras Shamayim*.

To return to our story, one young man had broken through many barriers on his descent from commitment to Torah. Among the non-serious, he was in a class by himself, being on an extra low level. From this low point, he lifted himself up, and on his ascent he passed the "serious crowd" and even some of the more dedicated individuals. Then he propelled himself from America to the European yeshivos and selected Slabodka, one of the most serious and intensive Torah centers. Here, Rebbe met him, and to top it all, he even wore his *tzitzis* out, a practice followed only by the most pious students. "Willie! What are you doing here?" the Rebbe spontaneously cried out. Willie warmly replied: "Remember that day we were coming down the corridor in opposite directions? As we were about to pass each other you remarked: 'Willie, when are you going to start taking life seriously?' Those words went straight into my heart like a dagger. They awakened me to the realization that I was tragically just wasting and ruining my life. This enlightenment led me step by step, through barrier after barrier, until I reached Slabodka, and here I am."

The Rebbe often explained that one should take advantage of any opportunity to communicate something positive. Once something is verbalized it makes an impression and has, in varying degrees, a definite effect. He used to say, "Once it goes down the hatch, it's there to stay."

The theory behind this principle is that every message that is picked up by one of our senses is recorded permanently in our brain cells, or, more accurately, in our soul. Every experience remains with us for our whole lifetime. The secular world is becoming aware of this phenomenon and has discovered that by electronically stimulating the brain cells, stored memories of life experiences can be accessed. Some of our great Torah sages—without electronic stimulation—recall being nursed by their mothers soon after birth. Even prenatal experiences are implanted in our memory.

The most stupendous insight our Sages impart to us on this topic is that even after we pass on, all our earthly experiences remain with us in the afterlife. The Rebbe cited as an example the episode related in *Masechta Berachos*, that a teenage girl who had passed away requested her cosmetics. These articles had been important to her during her lifetime and remained so even after she had passed on. The Rebbe also cited the incident told in the *gemara* of a few of the outstanding enemies of *Klal Yisrael* who had passed on and still spoke negatively about *Bnei Yisrael* despite their now being in the world of truth. They could not unshackle themselves from the false, wicked ideas by which they had lived. With this the Rebbe explained a puzzling *pasuk*: It is better to be confronted by a mother bear that has just lost her cub than by a fool with his foolishness (*Mishlei* 17:12). The ferocious bear is truly life-threatening, but at the very worst, she can only take someone from this world. On the other hand, if a fool imparts his foolishness to you, that registers in your mind and remains with you forever.

The Rebbe used this idea to explain the opinions quoted in *Pirkei Avos* as to the most important principle by which to live: according to one sage, it is having a good neighbor, and according to another, a good friend. More than the teachings of a rebbe, we are influenced by a neighbor because of the frequency of our exposure to him. And according to the other, this concept applies to a friend. In the same light, the greatest danger is to have a bad neighbor or friend, for the ultimate devastating effect is consistent exposure to a bad influence.

Lucky for you, Willie! It went right down your hatch.

CHAPTER TWENTY-THREE

Oranges, Apples, and Giraffes

*I*f I were asked to single out one specific area where the Rebbe especially excelled and exerted his broadest range of influence, I could unhesitatingly give the answer. It is what the *Sefer Chovos HaLevavos* calls *bechinah*, examining the creation to discern the wisdom and kindness of Hashem. This subject played such a dominant role in the Rebbe's life that a complete volume could (and should) be written, devoted to all the aspects of how the Rebbe delved into and spread this wisdom. However, to be loyal to our theme, we will have to suffice here just with some highlights.

It is not necessary to be guided by a Torah mandate when pure logic demands a certain behavior (*lama li kra, sevara hu*). However, aside from the fact that it is absolutely logical to look into the creation to see, understand, and appreciate Hashem's wisdom and greatness, there are also two clear Torah sources the Rebbe quoted for embarking on this endless, amazing voyage. Both the *Chovos HaLevavos* and the Rambam express the idea that the only way to come to recognize Hashem and to love Him is by examining the creation.

This subject has a very special significance for us here, since the walks we took were a fertile ground for its practical application. So many of the walks with Rebbe put *bechinah*, examination of the creation, into actual practice. The walks offered marvelous opportunities for observing a variety of aspects of the creation.

Typically, while walking the Rebbe would suddenly bend over and blow, sending gentle little puffs of dandelion heads into flight. He would then explain that each one was full of seeds which would eventually land somewhere to proliferate this species and to perpetuate its existence. Again the Rebbe would bend, and this time reappear with a propeller–like plant, marveling at how it takes off in flight, spinning like the overhead propeller of a helicopter, with a seed as its cargo. The Rebbe would go on and on, discovering the marvels of Hashem's creation, literally without limit, as it says, *"v'ligdulaso ein cheker*—to His greatness there is no limit"; it is infinite. The Rebbe could be addressing a group of learned Torah scholars and delving deeply, dissecting and analyzing an orange. Each aspect is a whole *sugya*, an independent subject: the outside peel, the color, the material, the rind, the meat, the pulp, and the seeds. The Rebbe delved into the animal world, disclosing the amazing Divine wisdom in every aspect of each creature. Without any reservation the Rebbe could indulge in a zoological discourse, describing the various physical features of the species and how marvelously they blend with the rest of the creation, how the bees are completely dependent on the plants to produce honey while at the same time the plant is completely dependent on the visit of the bees for the pollination process.

Man, the crown of creation, was one of Rebbe's main points of focus in displaying the infinite wisdom and goodness of Hashem. Wherever one turns, wherever one looks, the details upon details are so amazing, so breathtaking, that they almost seem like science fiction. One of the Rebbe's favorites was the mouth and the dental structure. Here we can openly see the marvels without having to go into the internal anatomy. The Rebbe would elaborate on how the front teeth act as scissors that cut the food to size. Next come the side teeth that slice the food further. Then come the molars that grind and pulverize. This process is orchestrated by the tongue, which at lightning speed is mobilizing the various morsels of food, each in its own stage, almost simultaneously. When the blending process is completed the tongue then proceeds to deliver the "goods" to the back section for the intricate swallowing process.

At that point in time the Rebbe was unique in this practice of making a considerable to-do of dissecting and analyzing the physical aspects of creation. As far as I know there was no one else in the Torah world who would indulge in such an endeavor. Does it seem right that a great Torah leader should stand before astute Torah students and lecture about the wiggling of the tongue? So despite the logic behind it, and the clear Torah sources that mandated it, at times I had inner doubts if this kind of discussion was really in the true Torah path of serving Hashem. Rebbe, Rebbe, please forgive me.

Then I discovered something that put an end to any shadow of doubt lurking within me as to the rightful respect I felt toward the Rebbe for the primacy of importance that he gave to this subject. The Steipler Rav was the undisputed *gadol hador*, the leader of the generation of the Torah world. This *gaon* was famous for his brilliance and greatness in Torah. His massive work, *Kehillos Yaakov*, shed light on whole areas throughout *Shas*. No one could compete with his diligence. People flocked to him for help with every difficulty, knowing that his *eitzos*, his advice, derived from *ruach hakodesh*, Divine inspiration, and his blessing and prayers brought constant salvation. The Steipler eventually produced a two-volume work called *Chayei Olam* revolving around the subjects of *yiras Shamayim*, character training, *hashkafos* (the proper Torah outlook), and inspiring a person to true diligence in Torah. In the second volume, Chapter 2, the Steipler quotes from the *Shaar HaBechinah* of the

Chovos HaLevavos and from the Rambam, both mentioned above, concerning the supreme importance of delving into the creation. Following this introduction, the Steipler proceeds without reservation to dissect and analyze the creation. For the remainder of the chapter he does not quote any *Chazal* or Torah sources, but just dives right into the anatomy. One of the first points of focus is the mouth, complete with the cutters, slicers, grinders, and the tongue. The holy Steipler does not refrain from pointing out that the giraffe, with its very unusual height, obtains the mainstay of its diet from treetops. Who would ever dream that the great Torah leader of the generation, the great *lamdan*, would think such thoughts? Who would ever dream that if he thought them, he would openly express them to anyone? Who would ever dream that he would commit them to writing, and have them printed in a *sefer*?

Continuing our walk, we pass a garden. We stop, and the Rebbe points out that with the correct approach, an observer can have as much pleasure from the garden as the owner who invested so much time and toil in it. A garden is there for us to embrace its beauty and enjoy. Then the Rebbe "digs in" and focuses on a flower to study, to appreciate, to be inspired by. How much inspiration? As previously related, the Rebbe once related that the greatest spiritual level he ever reached was by simple, focused, uninterrupted concentration on a flower. The colors—what beauty! Every petal is literally a work of art, and the scent—an open gift from Hashem that brings joy to our lives, as beautiful birds and fish do, too. Have we discovered a piece of *Gan Eden*?

Years later *"bechinah"* walks were organized in the country with the Rebbe. Imagine what treasures were found walking through the woods and mountain trails; had we discovered the whole of *Gan Eden*?

Giraffe munching from the treetops; can you top that?

CHAPTER TWENTY-FOUR

The Intrigue
Against Satmar

O n one memorable walk with the Rebbe I had a very unusual experience: the Rebbe shared with me some classified information. I am quite sure that at this point in time it is permissible for me to reveal it but I must first provide some background.

When the Rebbe accepted the position of *mashgiach* in Yeshivas Chaim Berlin and moved to New York, he found a typical Young Israel synagogue in his new neighborhood . These were men and women of strong character, the torchbearers of commitment to mitzvah observance in the modern generation. At the same time, unfortunately, since many were called upon to be the "breadwinners" or at least to supplement the family income, they were never the recipients of a full-scale Torah education as we know it today. As a result they were lacking in Torah knowledge and were ignorant in many important areas of halachah. At that time Torah was beginning to take root in America; authentic Torah-educated groups came to the States, and Torah institutions and yeshivos began to sprout and flourish. Unfortunately his congregation was not yet part of this spiritual explosion. On the contrary, they were drifting farther and farther away. More than once the Rebbe expressed to me his concern and great fear that many such congregations would soon drift outside the parameters of what we call Torah observance, similar to the Reform and Conservative movements. Torah-observant groups spanned the entire panorama from Satmar Chassidim, who were at the opposite end of the spectrum, to those who were marginally Orthodox.

The Rebbe was a clear, straight, committed Litvak, through and through. His path in Torah in no way smacked of Chassidus. This, however, did not deter him from agreeing with the Satmar way when he felt that they were right concerning specific issues.

I find it amazing that the Rebbe took upon himself the enormous challenge of uplifting, enlightening, and in a nutshell, accomplishing the major overhaul of these "modern" men and women. How the Rebbe managed this is a whole story in itself. What is relevant is that the Rebbe became, in effect, what was known at the time as an acting "Young Israel Rabbi." At that period of time, as we mentioned, there was a broad spectrum of groups bearing different *shitos*, mentalities, and opinions as to the correct approach to Torah. One of the Rebbe's greatest attributes was his *middah* of *emes*, that is, he was a relentless seeker of the truth. He cut through the obstacle course of convention and wherever he perceived there was truth, he focused on it and related to it.

However, the gap between the modern and the Satmar was growing wider and wider. Within the Torah-true camp, too, there raged major differences of opinion between Satmar and certain other groups, yet there was relative tolerance between them. R' Aharon Kotler, the recognized leader of one faction, once referred to the previous Satmar Rebbe, affectionately known as R' Yoilish, as follows: "He is one of the greatest of the generation both in Torah knowledge and general leadership, even though we disagree sharply on many issues." Likewise when R' Aharon passed away, the Satmar Rebbe left his sickbed against doctor's orders and insisted on being present at the *taharah*. At R' Aharon's funeral, which was attended by many thousands, he delivered a eulogy with bitter tears. In contrast, many lesser people, who unfortunately were Torah ignorant and had no real Torah leaders, were filled with bitterness and animosity toward Satmar. Through some channel unknown to me, word apparently reached the Satmar Rebbe of the respect and appreciation Rebbe had expressed for him on various halachic and leadership issues. I think this is sufficient background to understand and appreciate what followed.

The Rebbe received an urgent message that the Satmar Rebbe himself had a personal request to make of him. A certain organization was hosting a weekend in the Catskills, and the Satmar leadership had learned that certain elements in this group were planning to put none other than the Satmar Rebbe into *cherem*! The Rebbe was asked to do what he could to prevent this atrocity from taking place.

The amazing phenomenon in this incident was the confidence and trust the Satmar community placed in the Rebbe, who was so involved in and so much a part of American Orthodoxy.

As a point of interest, I once met an intelligent, educated fellow who was very much part of the Modern Orthodox, Zionist world, and who was obsessed with the desire to meet with the Satmar Rebbe to discuss their points of view. This meeting eventually came about, and this individual was absolutely amazed at the vast extent of the Satmar Rebbe's knowledge and familiarity with all the writings of the Zionist founders and leaders. Another point of interest is that the Satmar Rebbe was once seen to break down and weep upon hearing of some I.D.F. soldiers who had fallen in action. When questioned about this, he replied that he related to every Israeli soldier as his own son.

In my early youth I was *zocheh* to witness the sight of the Satmar Rebbe giving *chizuk* and rebuke before each *hakafah* on Hoshana Rabbah. It was an awesome experience: thousands of people relating to the day as it really is, a Yom Kippur. The sight of multitudes of grown, mature men crying like innocent children was something that I will never forget. I was told that my Rebbe, who usually did not venture anywhere outside of his set routine, eventually went to witness this awesome sight.

The Rebbe's *levayah* was attended by thousands of Satmar Chassidim, who had become sincere fans of his *sefarim* and tapes.

Thus the Rebbe served as a unifying force between the two extremes in the Orthodox world. The Rebbe never shared a follow-up on the distressing episode of the aborted *cherem,* but we never again heard of any attempts at carrying out such an outrageous intention.

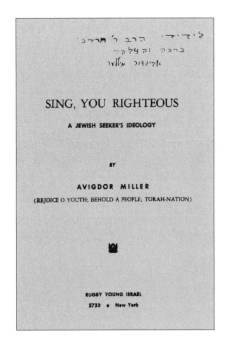

Rav Miller's personal inscription
to me in his sefer

Rav Miller and the author
in the 1950's

Rav Miller and the author before their last walk together

Rav Miller's haskamos to the author's "Don't Judge a Book by Its Cover"

Two journal messages dating back to the 1950's

*Rav Miller and Rav Scheinberg
at a wedding*

כאשר הכל כשול /ותבע/ אלוקים שלום,

ה' וברכה.

אל דברי לבבי שאו

שלום, בקרוב אל כול אל שבע

כאשר כתבתי כל הן, דבים רבים,

אך, צווי ותו לבי, חיים

הרוחני רצון כדן שאו יודע

מכולם דברי כל וכל כל

ואנחנו בים יאה שאון דברי אל

כזן אל גי, לומדי כא השאו

הראני אל.

ואנו שכתיר מו חמו אבן רק

בבוקר התחתינות צדין, ואנו אך

ואנו הכותנו אלג, כא הה כל

אל סמא אבוה כבוה אל כולב, אך

שבכבוד התחתינות, אלה כל שון כולם

כאשר אלה, אלב ול בלת אשן קוני

שלום דה, /אין כר כל פרות כאראנו,

אוירי,

אברהם ומרבן ופלץ

*Letter to Rav Chaim Dov Altusky
dating back to the 1960's*

Rav Miller's matzeivah

Rav Shmuel Miller being maspid.
The author is standing to the left of the speaker (1).

Rav Moshe Sternbuch speaking at Rav Miller's levayah in Eretz Yisrael.

At Rav Miller's kever on the yahrzeit. The author is standing on the right;
Rav Miller's son, R' Lazer, a Kohen, is standing on the pathway above the kever.

CHAPTER TWENTY-FIVE

Carnegie "Haul"

My walks with the Rebbe were, to say the least, inspiring, but they also were never lacking in surprises. I must say that surprises are often enjoyable; some say they are the spice of life. On the particular walk I have in mind, I had some especially good "spice."

One of the most vital areas in which the Rebbe enlightened us concerned various fallacies and expressions of covert wickedness in the ways of the non-Jews, their ideas, and their actions. The Rebbe had a special sensitivity and clarity that enabled him to perceive, single out, and crystallize the negative aspects of the customs of the non-Jews who surround us. This is obviously a vital matter, for we are in constant danger of having their mind-set infiltrate our value system. For example, many years ago there was a practice, even among our religious yeshivah students, that on public occasions, including weddings, bar-mitzvahs and shul functions, there was mixed dancing. This activity is obviously a severe transgression. What the Rebbe pointed out was that it was done by many who would never consider transgressing such a terrible *aveirah* as immodest behavior. At that time even many gentiles considered close physical contact indecent. Yet because it was labeled "social dancing" they allowed themselves— these decent, Torah-observant, upright men and women— to engage in this terrible transgression. It was the Rebbe's crystallization of the farce and the blindness instituted by the way of life of the non-Jews that was unique.

Because of this great danger of living in a non-Jewish environment, the Rebbe frequently pointed out the importance of keeping one's distance from gentile literature, education, and entertainment. With this background, imagine my surprise when, as we were walking, the Rebbe suggested that I read a secular book written by a gentile: Dale Carnegie's *How to Win Friends and Influence People*. A "chassid" would have run out and started reading the book before the Rebbe finished pronouncing the "D" of Dale. I, for some inexplicable reason, placed this striking suggestion in the category of things I would have to "get around to doing some day." The unusualness of the episode did not make very much of an impression on me until some time had elapsed and again I found myself on a walk with the Rebbe. You can imagine my shock when the Rebbe inquired as to whether I had read the book. This was a sufficient jolt for me to make a serious attempt to do so. After skimming through the seemingly boring, 1920's style of writing, I again allowed the goal of reading the book to slip away. With the whirlwind of life's events, getting married, and moving to *Eretz Yisrael*, I eventually forgot the entire matter.

Years later, I found myself *mashgiach* in a yeshivah in Yerushalayim. I was making the rounds, routinely checking the dorm rooms of what the Rebbe labeled the only spiritual oasis and "*ir miklat*" of our time, the yeshivah. I entered one of the rooms, and among this young man's literary collection I discovered Dale Carnegie's *How to Win Friends and Influence People*. In a flash, the memory of the whole episode with the Rebbe and his recommendation came to life. I was overcome with well-founded guilt feelings for being so callous and not being an obedient *talmid* and executing the Rebbe's wish quickly and enthusiastically. I was overjoyed at the thought that I could now get the book into my possession and have the opportunity to repent and faithfully fulfill the Rebbe's wish. I immediately located the owner and got his permission to borrow the book. I was resolved to read it through from the first letter to the last, no skimming, no skipping, and no skimping. I took upon myself with strong conviction and religious fervor the absolute obligation to meticulously read through the entire book. Having fulfilled my commitment, I found the book not as boring as I had thought it would be. Actually once you get into it, it is interesting and easy reading. After carefully going through the book I realized and understood what the Rebbe considered so exclusive, so vital, and so outstanding about it that he digressed from his usual way of doing things to share his enthusiasm with me and trouble himself with the follow-up reminder. Carnegie's great contribution, and what we have to gain, was his ability to open his readers' eyes to appreciate and really feel the issues he discusses. He actually opens your heart through his gift of bringing out his point in a way that hits home. He deals with very basic issues that affect the core of human relationships.

Everyone knows the difficulty we have in rebuking, criticizing, or in any way bringing sensitive issues to someone's attention. What is not commonly known, and what Carnegie enlightens us to, is the extreme extent to which even internally a person refuses to admit guilt and will constantly, consistently, and blindly fool himself with self-righteous cover-ups, justifying and rationalizing his wrongdoing. This is the typical human mentality and outlook, even if the act is decidedly wrong and/or the perpetrator himself is basically a dignified, refined individual.

Rashi on the *Chumash* quotes a most difficult *Chazal* which says that Yaakov Avinu delayed his rebuke to his sons, the holy *shevatim*, until the latest possible time before leaving this world. He did this because he feared that they would reject his rebuke, rebel, and defect to Esav's camp.

Carnegie opens our eyes to the need to make a great effort to understand and see things from the other person's perspective. In terms of the gratitude that we must feel and have toward our benefactors, his work is a masterpiece in teaching the arts of giving, understanding, and motivation. Mr. Carnegie winds up the book with seven chapters of advice for a happy, successful marriage, which are filled with the wisdom of life. Unfortunately the new, updated editions have deleted these chapters from the book, probably due to pressure from the women's liberation movement. This is a shame— get hold of an old edition.

I would again like to note that as much as I found true value in the points and the subjects that Carnegie touches upon, our Torah is certainly not lacking in a wealth of material on these matters. This leads me to one of the aspects of the book that disturbed me: Carnegie went to all ends of the universe to dig up sources for the points he makes. He quotes from the most remote documentation. Obviously, an enormous amount of serious, intensive research went into tracking down such sources. Unfortunately, however, we find an almost complete lack of any Torah source on these subjects. Considering the richness of the Torah on these matters and the serious research Carnegie put in, it would almost seem like an open, aggressive negativity toward that which is so sacred to us. The true reason for this omission never became known to me. Eventually, however, I saw in this a tremendous *hashgachah pratis*. First, it enabled the book to be read in locations where reading Torah is forbidden. Second, the book had a tremendous positive impact and influence on the world at large, even being translated into many languages. Included in the multitudes were probably many who were anti-Semitic, bearing hatred toward anything connected to Judaism. His great influence might therefore have been dampened had he quoted from Torah sources.

Eventually, after realizing how much I benefited because of the Rebbe's recommendation, I shared the book with others—friends, family, students, people involved in *chinuch*, running yeshivos and other institutions. Very positive feedback was given, and some said that the book had actually saved their marriages. Others claimed that it improved parent-child or teacher-student relationships.

I once was visiting with a renowned *rosh yeshivah* and *posek* and was toying with the idea of recommending the book even to this man of great stature. Imagine my surprise when I found it to be the only piece of secular literature in his home. Carnegie's "haul."[1]

Thank you, Rebbe.

---

1. I would like to share the following *hashgachah*. Recently an old *talmid* of mine called, unaware that I was writing these memoirs. He remembered that years back I had recommended the Dale Carnegie book, passing on the Rebbe's recommendation. He reported that he had heard a tape of one of the Rebbe's famous Thursday night *shiurim* (he did not recall the number). Someone asked the Rebbe if he recommended reading Dale Carnegie's book. The Rebbe replied that it was not necessary, since all the information there is available in our Torah. I don't know if Rebbe changed his viewpoint on the book, or whether his reply was meant specifically for this individual, or if he was simply cautious about making a public statement concerning Mr. Carnegie.

CHAPTER TWENTY-SIX

A Raid on Radar

*I*n *Chassidishe* circles, there is much emphasis and discussion regarding *inyanei kedushah*: maintaining purity of thought, keeping one's eyes focused properly, and related matters. In *Litvishe* circles the subject is taken no more lightly, to be sure, but it is dealt with in a different manner. It is not spoken about as openly or discussed often. We have in our tradition a number of stories about our *gedolim*, isolated incidents about their using different opportunities to express the proper outlook and to give *chizuk* on the subject. There are stories of some of our leaders devoting one talk every year to this matter. There is an incident regarding the Chafetz Chaim calling in one of his young sons for a talk on this topic. When he had completed what he had to say, he remarked to his son that he should keep this talk in mind, because it would not be delivered again.

The Rebbe, in the spirit of his *Litvishe* tradition, had a similar approach to this important matter, and refrained from addressing this issue as openly and often as is the practice among the Chassidim. Once in a great while, in speaking for a group of *bnei Torah*, he would address this matter of *kedushah*. Likewise, he would bring up the subject from time to time on an individual basis, to those who were close to him, in order to inspire, to direct, and to reinforce its importance.

Once while we were walking together, the Rebbe engaged me in such a session. He approached the subject by relating that on the previous day he had been walking in the street with an individual who had a reputation for being a learned person in Torah, who was well on in years, and I believe the Rebbe mentioned that he even sported a long white beard (which was not the norm in those days). The Rebbe related that it was a very unpleasant experience walking with him. He seemed to show a very obvious, unabashed interest in sights that he should really be avoiding. This person was really tied up with a strongly knotted rope, bound completely by the *yetzer hara*, who held this man helpless in its grip. The Rebbe expressed sincere pity for this poor fellow, so taken in by the *yetzer hara*. In an attempt to give a vivid description of how this individual appeared during his escapade of indulgence in scanning the scene, the Rebbe said that he resembled a radar screen, complete with its to-and-fro movements.

He explained that a lot of hard work must be invested to train ourselves properly in self-control of the eyes, particularly in regard to the challenges we experience in situations where there is a lack of modesty or related circumstances. A great majority of people neglect the proper training necessary. They do this under the pretense, rationalization, and error that as they grow older it is natural that this very tempting *yetzer hara* will surely and gradually release its grip. The truth is quite the contrary—as the person matures into his old age, the bad habits, if not previously checked, become more firmly established. The Rebbe explained the following extremely vital foundation. The time for one to actually begin working on himself and to have a serious self-training program is when he is a young *bachur*. One must train himself not to casually look around the street without any purpose. This applies even if the street is bare of anything immodest.

There is another common misconception regarding this premise that the Rebbe so wisely pointed out. Many make a mistake in thinking that even if they do not exert themselves, which is necessary for training in self-control, they will be released from all trials in this area when they marry. To quote the Rebbe, "They are under the false impression that marriage is an oasis from this lust, like an *ir miklat*." They mistakenly think that this was what *Chazal* meant when they labeled the status of marriage "*pas besalo*" (bread in one's basket): Since one has a sense of satisfaction and security because he has a wife, this insures him freedom from the *yetzer hara*. What *Chazal* were actually referring to, however, is a certain let-up in the intensity of the challenge, which can be helpful if accompanied by other precautions in keeping away from transgression.

The Rebbe pointed out that in *Chumash* we find the phrase, "they lifted their eyes and saw," regarding our forefathers. There is a definite connotation that they did not see anything until they made a specific effort to actually focus and see. They had developed themselves to the epitome of control, such that even after deliberately lifting their eyes, nothing registered without a special effort.

The *Mesillas Yesharim*, in Chapter 14, in discussing *perishus*—keeping one's distance from indulging in materialism—lists, among the ways of acquiring this state, not to look further than the radius of one's four cubits. For generations there were noteworthy individuals who lived according to this idealistic mentality and behavior. The famous R' Elyah Lopian *zt"l* came down very harshly on himself for unnecessarily looking up to see if a bus was coming just out of curiosity. This was in his ripe old age, when he was blind in one eye, and was on his way to the doctor, waiting impatiently for the bus to arrive so that he should not be late for his appointment.

R' Elyah was saddened, but the Rebbe had a lot of *nachas* from this champion of *shemiras einayim*.

CHAPTER TWENTY-SEVEN

Kollel and Soapsuds

The Rebbe and I passed a small supermarket in the course of one of our walks. A truck had pulled up and parked to make its delivery of detergent.

As we approached the Rebbe was surprised to find that he recognized the deliveryman. He greeted him warmly, but as he walked away his pleasant smile faded to distress and disappointment. What had caused this let-down?

The Rebbe explained that the last time he had seen him, this young man was a member of an illustrious, first-rate Kollel. He was learning with great diligence day and night, and was considered one of the most outstanding members of the Kollel. Now that he had completed many well-spent years of intensive learning, the Rebbe mused, he probably had a large family to support and a heavy financial burden. What could be objectionable in the nice, "clean" source of livelihood he had chosen? The Rebbe explained that there was absolutely nothing wrong with the type of livelihood he had chosen, for there isn't anything intrinsically negative or objectionable in blue-collar work, manual labor or, for that matter, any reputable means to earn an honest living, even for a *talmid chacham*. But here was a young man who had invested so much of his life for Torah, years of difficult toil, the complete, absolute devotion required of one who sincerely wants to learn Torah. The question was: all this personal investment and *mesiras nefesh*—to where did it all lead?

The Rebbe was disappointed because he felt that all that effort ought to have led to a more top-level, Torah-producing, purposeful end. This is as far as the fellow's personal investment was concerned. But what about the investment of *Klal Yisrael*, all the financial support that went into this young man's years of learning, which was sponsored by *Klal Yisrael* (this can include family members). Was this the expectation of the investors, that years of Torah learning should produce a soapsuds salesman? There was no shadow of a doubt that he did make a great effort to constructively maximize the Torah he acquired for the honor of Hashem and *Klal Yisrael*. The only reason he was not still occupied with this lofty ideal was because it was not Divinely decreed. Nevertheless, the Rebbe still felt that it was a cause for disappointment, considering all the effort invested.

What could be a creative course of action to rectify or improve such a situation? The advice the Rebbe gave was *tefillah*, to cry and appeal to Hashem that you want to continue your Torah learning in some form and at the same time have a livelihood. There is a very significant point that the Rebbe added here which can have an important impact on our lives in general. "*R'tzon yerei'av yaaseh*—Hashem fulfills the yearning of those who fear Him." This area of yearning is something we take for granted, since we feel that if we are praying for it, we must really want it. This is not always the case. Of course, at some level, we can say that we want it, but the question is, how badly do we really want it? How much does it truly mean to us? A person must work to generate within himself a most sincere feeling that he really *wants* to continue his learning. He has to have a clarity on his *hashkafos*, the correct mental attitude and motivation. He has to generate within himself a most sincere yearning and aspiration for his continued Torah learning.

The Rebbe went one step further—the objective is to *show* Hashem that this is really your will and yearning, and truly what you want. This is accomplished by learning to one's fullest capacity when the opportunity presents itself. Your yearning should be manifested in the form of open demonstration. This is accomplished by pursuing your priorities in the time that is available to you. By using your time to the utmost, you are appealing to Hashem to allow you to continue, by pursuing Him that this is what is important to you and what you really want. There are echoes here of the Mishnah in *Avos*, that a person who achieves in Torah under the stress of financial difficulties will in turn be Divinely blessed with the opportunity to continue to achieve in Torah under lavish monetary circumstances.

This is a unique concept, what the Rebbe called "prayer through action." Prayer is petitioning, declaring that you have a yearning for something. Prayer through action is doing the pleading by showing your yearning through action.

An outstanding and inspiring example of this was related by the well-known *Rosh Yeshiva* of Torah Ore, Rav Chaim Pinchas Scheinberg *shlita*. About sixty-five years ago, in his young years, the framework of his learning was the position he held as *mashgiach* in a yeshivah. It came to the point that it was impossible to support his family with the financial arrangement there. To leave the *beis medrash* and his learning, he felt, was absolutely not an option, and to stay was an impossibility. Caught in this complexity, he decided to put together a *sefer* on a subject in which he was well-versed, the *Ketzos HaChoshen*, as a possible source of income, even though in his general life plan it would never have occurred to him to write a *sefer* at that point in his life. Thus, he did not have to turn to the outside world as a source of livelihood, he stayed in learning, and his world-famous work, the *Tabaas HaChoshen*, came into existence.

The Rebbe's powerful thought about "prayer through action" can have profound influence and impact on the life and eternal existence of every one of us.

CHAPTER TWENTY-EIGHT

The Master (of) Peace

Once, at the outset of our walk, the Rebbe and I were victims of an actual ambush. Our *"attacker"* was a young fellow whose obvious objective was to engage the Rebbe in a debate that would escalate to the point of a sharp challenge, the goal being to "corner" the Rebbe into surrender. Then he would impose his outlook upon the Rebbe. Anyone of the Rebbe's stature would have had a right to express a strong negative reaction to this aggressive onslaught, and surely, justifiably so. Instead, the Rebbe put a warm hand on our young "attacker's" shoulder. Then, in a likewise warm voice and manner, the Rebbe reasoned with him that his whole agenda was not worth it. He explained to the young man that even if he scored a victory in the debate, he, the Rebbe, would not relinquish his present outlook. He ended in a humorous tone, saying, "I'm too old to change my ways, so it just doesn't pay." The "attacker" then put away his "weapons" and departed from us enveloped in the warm feeling radiated by the Rebbe's big smile. I feel fortunate to have been a witness to this masterpiece of interpersonal relations from a true master of peace. This situation, if allowed to take its natural course, would surely have ended in a vicious verbal battle resulting in bitterness and animosity on both sides. This sad ending, along with the many *aveiros* it would have entailed, was averted by the Rebbe's tact in his quest for peace.

A very similar incident occurred one Shabbos afternoon. Minchah was completed, and the Rebbe and the *kehillah* were about to commence *seudah shelishis*. The attention of the congregation was suddenly captured by the arrival of a young stranger. What really startled everybody was his announcement of his intention to deliver a *derashah* at *seudah shelishis*. To appreciate what transpired, one must keep in mind the true greatness of the Rebbe and the awe and respect the congregation had for him. The young man's presumption was an insult to the Rebbe and the *kehillah*. If this scene had taken its natural course, it would soon have turned into a fracas, complete with shouting, flaring tempers, and the young man finally being forcibly ousted from the premises, embarrassed and humiliated. The Rebbe quickly and diplomatically took charge of the situation, called the fellow over, and very warmly said to him, loud and clear, within hearing range of all those present: "You are really doing a great service to *Klal Yisrael* by going to shuls and speaking. The *rabbanim* are afraid to open their mouths, and the *kehillos* unfortunately hardly ever hear *divrei emes*, open expression of the Torah's truth. When you go and speak, you are giving these congregations at least some opportunity to hear true Torah values. In this shul, however, I am not at all inhibited about speaking the truth, loudly and clearly. This *kehillah* gets big doses of what they need to hear. So it is really not necessary for you to come here and speak. But we surely appreciate your good intentions." The young man walked away feeling "like a million dollars," not slighted, insulted, or rejected.

The Rebbe was unequivocally a straight Litvak and there was nothing "wishy-washy" about this. His acceptance of the *Chassidishe* groups, and his warmth toward them, were a result of his mentality, outlook, and way of life which emphasized minimizing dissention as much as possible. Another important point the Rebbe made about this matter was that disputes, differences of opinion, and *machlokos* that exist among the *gedolim* should be kept away from *baalei batim* as much as possible. These laymen usually misinterpret the dispute, as it seems to them that these giants are arguing about matters pertaining to the *yesodei hadas*, the basic foundations of Judaism and principles of faith. This in turn creates a weakening and deterioration of the followers' service of Hashem.

The unique stand of the Rebbe has special significance in this generation, which is plagued with so much dissention in general. The Rebbe made an all-out effort to combat this trend. In the framework of the many *shiurim*, *shmuessen*, classes, lectures, and *derashos* for both *bnei Torah* and the *baalei batim*, the Rebbe had many occasions to make reference to the *gedolei hador*, the Torah leaders of the generation. On these occasions he always mentioned them by name. On his list he never failed to specify clearly in one breath the *Chassidishe gedolim* right alongside the *Litvishe* leaders, not exhibiting any sign of priority or attributing any greatness to one over the other. The Rebbe used every opportunity to transmit this message. If he wanted to bring out a point using a story regarding the *gedolim*, he attempted, whenever possible, to include stories of the *Chassidishe manhigim* as well as the *Litvishe*.

The following is an example of a topic that the Rebbe spoke about in this light. The wonderful *zechus* of having the opportunity to be in close proximity to a *gadol* is well known and obvious. You are in a position to observe true greatness firsthand, with your own eyes. You discern subtle nuances that one can see only from close up. You may also have opportunities to converse, seek advice, or receive blessings, without hindrance of the red tape that sometimes makes access to the *gedolim* difficult. Additionally, you might be the recipient of a precious rebuke or having something brought to your attention about which you need to be enlightened. Being close to a *gadol* sometimes affords the opportunity to be of personal assistance and to serve him in some way. *Chazal* say that one can gain more by personally serving a *gadol* than by direct, structured learning.

There is, however, a negative side to all of this which is relatively unknown. In general, there is almost no positive situation from which an individual can gain that is not accompanied by a flip side that subjects one to unique dangers that he would not otherwise encounter. It is crucial that we view our *gedolim* with awe and esteem and relate to them as being on a "superhuman" plane, as they actually are. This outlook is the key to any connection one has with a *gadol* in any way. Being in close proximity, however, often breeds callousness which diminishes this awe and esteem, which in turn is detrimental to the true benefit to be derived from the connection. The point being, of course, how much we have to be on guard if we ever encounter this situation, to put up a resistance and not allow the familiarity to allow us to lose the proper esteem for the *gadol*.

To bring out this point of the danger of familiarity, the Rebbe had an anecdote which he cited on a number of occasions. The Rebbe once met a fellow who originated from a village that was home to a famous *gadol*. Upon being questioned by the Rebbe as to whether he had a connection with this Torah giant, the gentleman replied with a demonstrative hand movement: "Vat are you talking about? He lived right down my block." Whereupon he continued speaking about this *manhig,* whom he obviously cherished, but about whom he spoke with little reverence. At some points he even referred to this great leader only by his first name! The whole implication was … eh … that this *gadol* was not such a big deal.

Unfortunately, the issues revolving around the matter of Chassidim and *Litvishe* is generally misunderstood. There is generally an utter lack of clarity as to what exactly the opinions of the *gedolim* involved are. Often, a *gadol* is surrounded by satellites of *talmidim*, devoted students and *askanim*, people preoccupied with attending to all manner of affairs and projects that the *gadol* has planned or envisioned. Regrettably, the information they transmit sometimes does not accurately reflect the true opinions of the *gadol* they purportedly represent.

Receiving the news that a well-known *Chassidishe* leader had fallen sick, a *Litvishe rosh yeshivah* who was considered an opponent of his was affected to the extent that he nearly collapsed from distress. Subsequently, he was questioned by his close followers about this reaction. He explained that his disagreement was with certain ideological principles of this group, but he had nothing at all against the leader personally. Here again we see error and confusion. The followers were mistaken in thinking that their leader was waging a war against the *Chassidishe* leader. They, in turn, as devoted followers, carried out their loyal obligation, taking up the "cause," as a personal conflict against the leader, until they were fortunately enlightened by their *rosh yeshivah*. Until then, however, this group was tragically living in the blindness of their misconception.

Disagreement in Torah or in principles can be a healthy phenomenon, as we see with regard to the *machlokes* between Hillel and Shammai. The trouble comes when the disagreement revolves around issues that are not really issues, differences that do not exist, or when the disagreements deteriorate and turn to hatred, animosity, and antagonism. This is what the Rebbe was campaigning against, and to this end the Rebbe certainly did well.

CHAPTER TWENTY-NINE

Conventional

Unconventionalism

*A*mong the most beautiful aspects of the Torah is the fact that despite the defined, circumscribed, rigid structure of the mitzvos, Hashem in His infinite wisdom has provided room for personal development and movement, for the unique creativity of the individual personality. As a general life pattern, our leaders, the *gedolim*, encourage keeping to a middle path, adapting to a conventional way of doing things. They encourage us not to deviate from the ways of the *tzibbur*. A person's mentality and outlook should be to follow the conventions of the *rabim*, the majority. This was surely the Rebbe's way. The Rebbe, we can say, was an outstanding substantiation of the principle of conforming and refraining from being a deviator from the trodden path.

The beauty of it all, as we pointed out, is the freedom allowed within the conformity. The Rebbe likewise was an amazing example of the balance of conventionalism with originality, creativity, and flexibility.

There is an old saying that things are hidden from us by being right under our noses. On the walk I will now share with you, the center of attention is something under our noses which we have not focused on as of yet, namely, *the walk itself.* Daily walks are an activity which have always been enjoyed by many. However, in recent years, medical science has discovered and continues to disclose countless benefits in this precious exercise. As a result, today it has become a very popular pastime; it has become part of the mind-set of a broad sector of the population. The Rebbe, however, was living at a time when all this was a relatively unknown practice. His walking program was really something unusual and unique for the times. To the Rebbe the walking was a serious undertaking, carried out every single day, without any exception, whatever the weather conditions. The priority he gave to it could also be seen by the serious amount of time that he allotted for it daily, and by the distance he covered in each walk.

True, people always did walk; husband and wife indulge in an evening stroll. How could anyone miss the Friday night or after-the-*cholent* promenade, or for that matter the "after the temper tantrum" cooling-off hike? But to be committed to such a regimented routine and to adhere to it religiously—days, weeks, months, and years for over half a century—can only be carried out by pure unconventionality.

Today we are living in an era of *kiruv rechokim*, structured, organized reaching out to the spiritually needy. This is the age of SEED programs: top level, exceptional yeshivah students from outstanding Torah centers and Kollels infiltrating communities far removed from *Yiddishkeit* in remote areas worldwide. They have intensive learning programs of their own; they maintain outstanding scholastic achievements while simultaneously engaging in very effective outreach programs to communities at large. Yeshivos always existed in *Klal Yisrael*, but the synthesis of serious yeshivah learning and *kiruv* was not commonplace until very recently. There was one exception to all this, one beautiful ray of light in a dark, dark world. Over half a century ago, in the early 1950's, the Rebbe—then deeply engrossed in his Torah learning and steeped in the yeshivah world in the role of *mashgiach* in one of the most intensive, outstanding yeshivos of the time—took a "giant step" and stretched out his hand to the layman's world, which was far from Torah-true observance. In his own version of a "seed" outreach program, he succeeded in his unconventional, original way in influencing this community to reach new heights and become one of the most outstanding Torah *kehillos* of our time. How is this for independence and uniqueness?

The American yeshivah students who went to study in European yeshivos in the 1930's were certainly independent individuals. For an adult young man to take his Torah learning seriously was a rarity in those days. And to be inspired to travel to Europe to the great yeshivos was something done only by the elite of the elite. The Rebbe, however, was already a qualified teacher with a degree and a license, and was prepared and ready to start a career. For someone at that stage of his life to travel to Europe in pursuit of advancing his Torah studies, can only be the actions of a completely independent non-conformist.

Beginning in the 1950's the Rebbe had small groups, or *vaadim*, of yeshivah students from the greater New York area that met regularly. The existence of this network was considered secret, classified information to the extent that one group did not even know about the other. (I was aware of this project because I had the *zechus* to be personally involved in helping the Rebbe in its organization, and I would assume at this point that it is no longer confined to secrecy.) The function of these groups was a concrete program of growth in all areas of *avodas Hashem*. Each unit was a "workshop" with the input and participation of its members. Each member had to give an account to the group, and in some groups the members were required during the course of the week to mail a postcard to the Rebbe with a progress report. How is this for unique originality?

The Rebbe took the members of his congregation (and eventually anyone who wished to join his study groups), laymen who were ignorant of *any* Torah knowledge, and slowly and systematically raised them to the point where they had a strong knowledge of many tractates of *Shas*. This serious program meant being tested, and being responsible to know the information. It is hard to fathom, but there were *baalei batim* who actually completed and were tested on the *entire Shas*. How is this for originality and unique creativity!

Our list could go on and on; I guess the selection of this subject matter is itself quite original, if I may say so.

CHAPTER THIRTY

Parlez-vous Yiddish?

hazal tell us that one of the three factors that made our forefathers worthy of redemption from the bondage of Egypt was that they retained their mother tongue, *lashon hakodesh*. The conventional way of understanding this is in the framework of reward. For the merit of clinging to the holy language in a foreign land, they were rewarded with redemption. This is logical; however, it is also probable that specific, special, and important aspects of the language contributed to making *Klal Yisrael* worthy of the great redemption. Speaking a specific language demonstrates a strong commitment to an identity.

My walks with the Rebbe did not lack surprises, and one promenade I am thinking of had a special one. As we were walking the Rebbe stopped abruptly, looked me in the eye and said: (I would just like to point out that it had nothing to do with the subject we were speaking about, and as the old saying goes—it was as if it fell from "outer space.") "From now on," the Rebbe said, "all our communication with one another will be solely in Yiddish." He then added, "This is more befitting the full-fledged "Mirrer Yeshivah *mahn*" you are now." I was a young teenager when I first met the Rebbe. I went through various stages and metamorphoses in the course of the years I knew him, and I eventually entered the Mirrer Yeshivah. It seems that the original impression he had gotten of my being a young, red-blooded teenager still remained with him. Speaking Yiddish would help provide me with the right perspective.

The fact that I was in a position to follow the Rebbe's request, instruction, or demand, was in itself a story. From where was I supposed to have a workable knowledge of Yiddish (a language which, in that time, in our circles, was obsolete for all practical purposes)?

In 1958 I entered the Mirrer Yeshivah in Brooklyn. The *rabbanim* there were among the greatest *lamdanim* of the illustrious Mir of old. I had the *zechus* to be in the *shiur* of HaRav Elya Yurkansky *shlita*. "R' Elya," as he is known, is one of the outstanding *talmidim* of the famous *rosh yeshivah* and great leader, R' Elchanan Wasserman, *hy"d.* R' Elya, like the other *rebbeim*, spoke only Yiddish. The *shiur* consisted of a fine group of boys who, like me, had very little knowledge of the language. The material was certainly not a barrage of sweet Yiddish niceties and salutations, or old tasty Baranovich potato kugel recipes. In technical, or secular, terms it was an in-depth, complex analysis of Talmudic texts that were complicated to begin with. All this, however, was presented in a way that actually sounded delectable, enjoyable, and inviting. R' Elya's delivery was with great excitement, radiating enthusiasm. He created in us a yearning and appetite to understand. This burning desire is the only logical account that can be given for our having been able to overcome such a great communication gap. There was not only the ability to comprehend the delicate nuances of subtle differences, but also the ability to communicate with R' Elya. This was so amazing that it was an inexplicable phenomenon. This experience was responsible for my knowledge of usable Yiddish and explains how I was able to acquiesce to the Rebbe's wishes.

R' Elya (in 2003) still maintains the same position as *maggid shiur* in the Mir and continues inspiring his *talmidim*; Hashem should give him health and strength to continue for many more years to come. (In 1983 we had the honor of hosting R' Elya and his Rebbetzin during their visit to *Eretz Yisrael*.)

Although we have gone off on a tangent, this little deviation really brings us back to the Rebbe. Yeshivas Mir eventually discovered the Rebbe, and invited him to give *shiurim*. It was in this framework that HaRav Shraga Moshe Kalmanowitz *zt"l* became closely acquainted with the Rebbe and arranged that he give his Thursday night class for the Flatbush Sephardic community. This ultimately became the Rebbe's greatest channel of influence to the world. The class itself, which eventually was given at the Rebbe's own shul, was attended by many for years. The *shiurim* were recorded on cassettes and were disseminated literally around the globe, exerting the Rebbe's influence on thousands throughout the world. Many multitudes, because of the strong influence these *shiurim* had on their lives, consider themselves close followers and *talmidim* of the Rebbe.

The request of the Rebbe for me to speak Yiddish really was a demonstration of how I should distance myself from the manners, mentality, and mode of communication of the society in which we were living. However modest and small, it was a much-needed effort to resist the influence of our perverted, destructive surroundings.

Speech is a double-edged sword. On the one hand it is an indicator of, and on the other hand it has an influence on, a person's character. Speech reflects and reveals much about a person. I had the tremendous *zechus* to be a guest at the Rebbe's Seder table. The insight I gained about the Seder from this experience is immeasurable. The Rebbe's general approach to all Torah was to achieve clarity, to understand things in the simple truth of their meaning. Occasionally he allowed himself what is referred to as a "*drush vort,*" a thought based on a play of words, deviating from the simplistic meaning. One such example was the selection he repeated in the name of his own *rebbeim*. The *Haggadah*, in making reference to the four types of sons, says: *"Chacham mah hu omer?*—What does the wise one say?", and then goes on to explain. It does likewise with the other three types of sons. The *"drush vort"* was to punctuate the sentence differently—*"Chacham mah hu? Omer";* i.e., a wise man exhibits his nature in the way he expresses himself.

On the other side of the coin, our speech has an awesome, far-reaching impact on our character and has a profound influence on our outlook and mentality, as well.

Until recently, even among gentiles there was a strict code of communication values. From the highest level of society to the simplest layman, they maintained a way of speaking and writing that had a specific standard of abstaining from vulgarity. This had a profound influence on them and on the world at large. Presently, we are living in an era quite the opposite, and likewise, unfortunately, the "boomerang" effect is indeed catastrophic. Society, being at an extremely low point, condones the worst communication standards, which in turn has an even more devastating effect on its essence. *Klal Yisrael*, living in *galus,* is most definitely affected. One aspect of this corrupt communication, aside from the vulgar vocabulary, involves the taunts and the sarcasm that emanate from one to another. In the normal course of speech people are encouraged to think of the most hurtful thing they can say to their best friend or closest relative. For example, if a dear friend is overweight, it is common to poke fun over it, especially if the subject is sensitive about the issue, and people actually do this in public. The poor victim then makes an all-out attempt to return the onslaught, and if he is "lucky," the attacker may have a defect that he can use to really get back at him. The baseness of this quite reckless, inconsiderate behavior has unfortunately infiltrated our circles and it is justified with the rationalization that it is all under the banner of banter—light-hearted, humorous jest. From a halachic viewpoint the leniency that is relied upon is that "nobody is *makpid"*—meaning they do not stand on the rights that protect their pride and self-respect. *Rabi U'Mori HaGaon HaRav* Chaim Pinchas Scheinberg *shlita* made an important observation regarding this halachic rationalization. He pointed out that when one is the recipient of insults and is deeply hurt, especially when one is publicly embarrassed, very often, if not always, the victim does not truly forgive, but because it is all part of the social game he must play in order to be accepted, he does not in any way exhibit this hurt. It is almost certain, however, that the victim is so emotionally wounded that in his heart he does not forgive.

This whole mentality and behavior is totally against the principles of *Klal Yisrael* and even decent human behavior. We believe that a person should always think of what he can say or do to bring good feelings and happiness, and to raise the self-esteem of every human with whom he comes in contact.

The whole attitude regarding communication in general, that there is a need for incessant speech when in the presence of another person and that silence, even for a brief lapse of time, is "uncomfortable," is diametrically opposed to the Jewish concept in this area. The Rambam says that a person should relate to the subject of expressing oneself and speaking in the same manner as he would if he were spending money.

In contrast to this verbal pollution in which we find ourselves today, our language is called *lashon hakodesh*, we were taught, because it has no nouns for the reproduction organs. It is said that the language of Yiddish was created by our *gedolim* as a holy language for *Klal Yisrael* to use in the course of our exile.

At the Rebbe's *levayah*, here in *Eretz Yisrael*, his son R' Shmuel related in his eulogy that one of the Rebbe's last requests was that his family, his children, grandchildren, and great-grandchildren should communicate in Yiddish. It seems that the Rebbe considered me a member of the family.

A dank, Rebbe, az ihr hut mir oisgelernt tzu reden vi a Yid darf reden.

CHAPTER THIRTY-ONE

Walks for Talks

hazal tell us that there were families in *Klal Yisrael* (including some who were *Kohanim*) that acquired high-level, sophisticated talents for themselves in assorted areas. They guarded their techniques as classified information. The Rebbe, who was also a *Kohen*, had become very accomplished and developed a highly sophisticated talent in the field of public speaking. He did not try to keep this art a secret, however, and on the contrary, had the aspiration and desire to share it. On one of our walks I had the privilege and honor of having the Rebbe begin to share it with me.

In order to comprehend and appreciate the magnitude of the Rebbe's awesome talent in this field, it is important to comprehend that it was through this power of speech that the Rebbe managed to accomplish the positive upheaval of a whole community. He did it with great wisdom and patience, but the Rebbe's main tool of influence was his magnificent *derashos*. Among all the various *shiurim*, classes and "lectures" the Rebbe gave, including the famous Thursday night talk, the Shabbos afternoon *Aggadata* class and the *Chovos HaLevavos* group, there was nothing comparable to the Shabbos morning *derashah*. I find it impossible to describe exactly what it was; however, I shall make an attempt. The Shabbos morning *derashah* was an experience, not just an enlightening *shiur* but an experience. It is the only time I heard a speech that was so completely captivating that I would lose awareness of everything but the Rebbe and what he was saying. When the *derashah* was completed it actually took a while to "get back" and I had to remind myself as to my whereabouts. The Rebbe cast this "spell" through his great oratory talents. All this was accomplished with a most delicate selection and manipulation of voice, volume, pitch, vocabulary, and expressions. This was the Rebbe's super-vehicle for creating the great upheaval and transformation.

There were many issues that needed an overhaul, some of which were really basic matters touching on the very foundations of our faith. Despite the urgency, carefully calculated timing was crucial. The Rebbe indeed bided his time, scrutinizing and constantly sizing up the readiness of the congregation to see whether the time was ripe to broach one of these pressing issues.

This is reminiscent of the story the Rebbe himself related concerning the time R' Yisrael Salanter spent a Shabbos in a certain European seaport city. The population there made their livelihood from the boats that docked each week on Shabbos. After the Shabbos morning "services," they all rushed to their special weekly Shabbos work. Being present at their Shabbos service, R' Yisrael was honored by them with a request to speak, which he declined. Upon visiting the community at some later date he was again honored, and this time he obliged and addressed their *chillul Shabbos* with a most clever approach. The Rebbe elaborated on the reason R' Yisrael had refrained from speaking on his earlier visit and the self-control he had exercised because he felt it was not the right time. When R' Yisrael finally did address them he did so with great success, and step by step, he eventually brought the entire city to complete *teshu-vah* and *shemiras Shabbos*.

The Rebbe's high-caliber speaking talents included his flawless diction, pronunciation, and voice modulation. Added to this was his perfect English grammar, sentence structure, vocabulary, and choice of words. I perpetually marveled at this phenomenal perfection: if one of the Rebbe's *derashos* were to have been written down word for word as he spoke, it would have made a stunning piece of literature.

All this certainly does not complete the story of the Rebbe's massive spiritual overhaul. It is only intended as an insight into the quality and power of the Rebbe's verbal surgery.

So on this very special walk the Rebbe shared his advice and directives on the art of public speaking. He presented me with down-to-earth, practical exercises for developing and fine-tuning my public speaking abilities. I will share one very precious, helpful piece of advice I received. Every day, take a selection of reading material in English and read it out loud for five minutes at a pronounced, exaggeratedly slow speed, carefully enunciating every syllable. One will detect within a short duration of time the positive effect this has on one's speaking performance.

In the framework of sharing his superb understanding of this art, the Rebbe eventually put together a group of his close *talmidim* for the purpose of developing our public speaking abilities. This was a most unique and unusual undertaking for someone of the Rebbe's stature. At our meetings, he had us take turns speaking before the group, and everyone present, including the Rebbe himself, had to give feedback, comments, and criticism on each speech. Can you imagine the magnitude of this act? Imagine a person of such stature, whose every moment was so precious, devoting time and effort to patiently observing our performance, listening attentively and contributing constructive criticism and fine tuning. His helpful comments covered both our subject matter and our performance. Eventually he honored each of us with the opportunity to speak at *seudah shelishis* before the whole congregation in the presence of the Rebbe, and on this speech, too, we received his very precious comments.

Usually I had talks on the walks with the Rebbe; today it was certainly a walk for the talks.

CHAPTER THIRTY-TWO

Rugby

How is it possible to reflect on walks with the Rebbe without focusing on the Rebbe's congregation? How can anyone think about the Rebbe's life without connection to his *kehillah*? Because of the dominant role it played in the Rebbe's life, the *kehillah* was very frequently our subject of conversation on our walks together. An adequate presentation of this subject, giving it the space it deserves, could fill many volumes. With the utmost esteem, and begging forgiveness of the Rebbe and the *kehillah* for not paying the full respect due, I wish to present a quick reflection of that golden era when the Rebbe inspired, uplifted, and altered the mind-set, outlook, and daily life of a young, strong-minded, vibrant community. Dedicated and devoted to the ideals they held, and exposed to the Rebbe's powerful influence, they allowed his fiery messages to infiltrate their value system, resulting in a dynamic transformation that covered the full spectrum of their lives. Let us quietly sneak a glimpse into the window of the little old Rugby Shul on East 49th Street and bend our ears to the goings-on.

The Rebbe's shul comprised a congregation that is known today as an outstanding, model Torah community. Its uniqueness as a *kehillah* of laymen who are highly accomplished in Torah scholarship and mitzvah observance is widespread, common knowledge. There is an aspect of this, however, that is hardly known, and that is the roots of this *kehillah*. This outstanding Flatbush group actually had its origins in East Flatbush, in a neighborhood known as Rugby. It was part of a worldwide network of Orthodox shuls known as Young Israel. During the 20th century, with the great spiritual devastation taking place in the United States, this network served as a tremendous source of spiritual inspiration. It presented a great motivation for the youth to remain loyal to the Torah. How fortunate these souls were to be saved from the wholesale assimilation and spiritual destruction that was rampant. Many of them deserved to be classed among the great, lofty spiritual heroes of the times, because they kept their commitment and loyalty to the religion of their forefathers.

Strange as it may seem, however, although they were so staunchly committed, at the same time the major pillars and foundations of our religion were in a state of decay among these communities. Most of their members were lacking a concrete Torah education; they had almost no real knowledge of, or even ability to study, Torah. Another most vital area in which they were lacking was Torah leadership. Because they lacked it, they also lacked an understanding of the crucial role it plays. Consequently, many members never sought real Torah leadership, nor did they have proper respect and reverence for rabbinical authority. Their actual fulfillment of the laws was on a very modest level, and unfortunately filled with many inconsistencies. The level of observance among the branches of Young Israel varied, and I was told by old-timers that the Young Israel of Rugby, as it was known, was on one of the lowest levels in the movement.

Whenever the Rebbe felt the time was ripe, he would select an issue that needed to be addressed and embark on a campaign for change by means of the Shabbos morning *derashah*. He would start by introducing the issue gently and bring it up again several weeks later. He would continue in this way, gradually building up to a crescendo which was marked by the delivery of what I called his "atomic explosion." The Rebbe's success rate was very high, as can be deduced from the constant upgrade in the quality of the *kehillah*.

■ *No Carrying or Smoking Allowed*

He would deal in this way with carrying on Shabbos, which was a commonplace transgression at that time. In the final stages he would deliver fiery *derashos* on the subject, making statements like, "It is worse to walk to shul with a handkerchief in your breast pocket on Shabbos than to smoke a cigarette," which the public understood was strictly forbidden, and they were shocked and horrified by the statement. He would later explain that carrying in a public domain is unanimously considered a full-fledged *melachah*, in contrast to *havarah* (smoking), on which there is a difference of opinion.

■ *Kosher Meat Can't Be Beat*

On another occasion the Rebbe judged that the time was now ripe to censure the patronizing of butcher shops with unacceptable *kashrus* standards. The same pattern was employed, starting with a series of low-key *derashos* and gradually building up to powerful verbal weaponry. A statement was made that put the whole neighborhood in an uproar after it was published in the local newspaper: "By feeding your children meat purchased in stores with unreliable supervision you will be making them into criminals." The Rebbe was of course referring to the *timtum halev* referred to by *Chazal* in their teaching that consuming forbidden food exerts a corrupting force on our value system. The campaign was successful, like all the others.

■ *To Be or Not T.V.*

Today even secular sources decry the destructive force of television in the home. The Rebbe was a pioneer in opening the eyes of the public long before this negative influence was popularly recognized. "A septic tank, pouring out into your living room!" he cried out in one of his later, stronger sermons. In his *Shabbos HaGadol derashah* which is conventionally devoted to the laws of Pesach, he warned the *kehillah* that when searching the house for some tiny *chametz* crumbs with a candle, they should be sure not to overlook the "gigantic hunk" of *chametz* in the living room, suggesting they make *biur* on it with a large hatchet. Concerning some of the popular T.V. stars he commented, "Would you ever consider allowing a despicable low-life into your home to sit in your living room and entertain your family?" In this, too, the Rebbe proved a success, and a great number of homes became "purified."

■ *The Philosophy of Phylacteries*

Another area which was a complete disaster was the mitzvah of *tefillin.* The style then was that when one reached bar-mitzvah a pair of *tefillin* was purchased at the average cost of about $5; even in those times when money had greater value, it is not probable that one could acquire a pair meeting even minimal *kashrus* requirements for that sum of money. Following this ridiculous purchase, the pair was usually worn by its owner for his whole lifetime, never getting the minimum conditioning that even the best, high-quality *tefillin* need from time to time. The cost of a good pair of *tefillin* in those days was from 50 to $100, comparable to a pair that would cost about $1,000 today. Can you imagine the scene at the Young Israel of Rugby upon the Rebbe's successful completion of his *tefillin* campaign? To walk in and see a congregation of simple laymen almost all wearing beautiful, shining, *mehudar*, $100 *tefillin*—what a sight!

Dancing Around the Hadassim Bush

■ In those days the Rabbi and the *shammos* were the sole individuals who had in their possession the four *minim* used on Succos; it almost seemed improper for anyone else to possess them. Yet, through the influence of the Rebbe's *derashos*, the whole congregation made the rounds of *Hoshanos* and the *naanuim*, each worshiper with his own four species. This is a sight that we are familiar with and accustomed to today. For those times, however, it was a most spectacular scene.

- *A Guest of Honor for the Nights of Honor*

True fulfillment of the mitzvah of *succah* was absolutely non-existent. Many shuls had *succos*, where a small number of the extra-devout would make *Kiddush* and leave. With his fiery words, the Rebbe inspired his congregants to feel a desire for the real mitzvah. Next, they had to be motivated to arrange a suitable location on their property, and finally, to do the actual work of building. Not having the necessary skills in carpentry and construction needed for *succah* building, it was predictable that many of the congregants would be the recipients of hard blows on their thumbs or other organs, and as a result would come to shul bearing obvious medical dressings. The Rebbe, in one of his inspiring sermons, exclaimed that any bandages from *succah*-building wounds are badges of glory and honor, designating their wearers as knights of valor, among the heroes of the Succah Pioneers Brigade. Realizing how difficult a challenge it would be to fulfill this mitzvah, the Rebbe felt that he should offer a special incentive. At the "nuclear" *derashah* he announced something extremely unusual and wondrous. Everyone and anyone who successfully put up a *succah* in their home could expect a personal visit from the Rebbe at their *succah*.

- *Put Your Account Where It Counts*

The Rebbe initiated a campaign concerning *tzedakah*—how much and to whom it should be given, which was a bone of contention. In these circles, unfortunately, monies were often directed to causes that were literally against the Torah. Eventually the Rebbe got the *baalei batim* to contribute to the best Torah centers in the world and the finest causes in *Klal Yisrael*. The Rebbe explained that the greatest tragedy that can befall a Jew, even worse than transgressions, is to arrive at the next world thinking that he has brought a treasure of mitzvos with him, only to discover that his *tzedakah* has been discounted because he donated to the wrong causes.

- *Do Your Horah in Honor of the Torah*

Simchas Torah is a time of joy for our accomplishments in Torah and for expressing our most sincere gratitude to Hashem for giving

us the Torah. I will attempt to depict how the day was usually cele-
brated in these circles of laymen. The most sophisticated and dignified adults spent the day occupied with absolutely ridiculous absurd-
ities, acting completely foolish to a background of senseless jokes
and bufoonery. The youngsters pulled pranks that entailed monetary
loss and disrespectful treatment of holy articles. It took a tremendous amount of verbal effort on the Rebbe's part to create a reversal
and to put things in their proper perspective. He was eventually successful in establishing the atmosphere of a real *makom Torah*, with
"serious" *simchah*. The Rebbe kept a constant watch for any breach
and would stamp out any beginnings of the old nonsense. The Rebbe
himself would very actively lead the singing and lively dancing.

■ *Toirah Iz Die Beste Schoira*

Among his greatest accomplishments was that he got the membership to remove their children from inferior educational institutions and enroll them in the best yeshivos available for boys and
girls. Besides the fact that the children were receiving a top quality Torah education, producing a new generation of first-class
Torah citizens, they also had a strong influence on their parents,
causing a "sandwich" effect. The congregants now had their children coming home bearing Torah-true values on the one hand,
and on the other hand there was the influence and input of the
Rebbe. The Rebbe accomplished all this through his extraordinary
oratory talents.

In his effort to inspire the *baalei batim* to strive for the goal that
their children become great in Torah, the Rebbe related the following thought—one of the most beautiful I ever heard from the Rebbe.
Chazal tell us that Yaakov Avinu's twenty-two years of suffering—
when he was separated from his son Yosef and was under the mistaken impression that Yosef had been fatally attacked—was a Divine
retribution. Yaakov was being punished for the twenty-two years that
he was absent from the house of his father, Yitzchak Avinu, and consequently failed to fulfill his obligations of *kibbud av*. *Chazal* then
point out that he was actually separated from his father for thirty-six
years, adding the years that he was in the yeshivah of Shem and

Ever. Why weren't these years included in the punishment? They explain that Yaakov Avinu was not considered negligent in fulfilling the mitzvah of *kibbud av* during these years that he was studying in the yeshivah since his Torah learning was considered the proper thing to do.

An obvious question presents itself: Yaakov's taking leave of his father's presence was originated by his mother Rivkah, who was guided by Divine inspiration; besides, he was forced to flee since Esav was seeking to kill him. The Rebbe presented the following answer in the name of his mentors, interjecting that it was consistent with the Slabodka approach to understanding *Chazal*. There is no question that Yaakov Avinu's taking leave of his father was the proper thing to do. The criticism placed on Yaakov Avinu was something very subtle. He surely acted properly by leaving his father's presence; however, he was lacking in the degree of frustration and heartache he should have felt at being in a predicament that prevented him from giving his father the honor he deserved and bringing him joy and happiness. Another question now arises: since it turns out that both the years Yaakov was away at Lavan's house and the years that he was learning in the yeshivah of Shem and Ever were mitzvos and both the proper thing to do, and that Yaakov's only guilt was for not feeling a proper degree of anguish at not being with his father, he should have had to answer for this claim against him no matter where he was. Now it is truly a wonder why the years Yaakov was at Lavan's house were singled out for retribution.

On this the Rebbe explained that when Yaakov was in Lavan's house the fact that he was deprived of the ability to serve his parents the delicacies they appreciated or to clean their house was something that certainly deserved his remorse. However, when Yaakov Avinu was in the yeshivah learning Torah, said the Rebbe, there was absolutely no place for remorse, regret, or sadness. The most wonderful thing a child could ever do for his parents is learn Torah. Should he have been sad that he could not be at home to wash the floor? The greatest act of kindness, the greatest favor, the grandest gift that one can give his parents is to learn Torah.

With this *derashah*, the Rebbe certainly motivated everyone to aspire to have their children steeped in Torah studies.

Of all the Rebbe's accomplishments with the *kehillah*, the greatest and most significant was in this area of Torah study. Because this achievement was so spectacular, however, and also because Torah is in its own class, this subject deserves a chapter of its own.

■ *Yes, Lip Service*

One of the most vital areas in which the *baalei batim* needed a major overhaul was *davening*. It is important to emphasize again that these people were among the Jewish heroes of their time; any area in which they were lacking was certainly not due to their negligence, but to the general lack of access to proper religious education. The very first issue that had to be dealt with was something very basic indeed: the moving of one's lips. In our secular education, we had all been trained not to move our lips while reading. The teachers were quite adamant about this rule and sharply criticized any student who transgressed it. "Read with your eyes, not with your lips," was drilled into them. Not only was it considered wrong to produce a sound but even just silently to move one's lips was a grave sin.

Among the great secrets of the universe, and something of which the secular world was ignorant, is that the movement of the lips, the participation of the vocal chords, or the dynamic involvement of the limbs intensifies, upgrades, and enhances considerably the quality of the learning process. *Chazal* relate that one of the great *chachamim* periodically did a mental review of everything he had acquired in his Torah studies. Unfortunately, he did not retain his learning and it was all forgotten. He was advised to enunciate the words he was learning. This activated his memory, and he then began to retain all his knowledge. It was quite natural, however, for the American-educated *baalei batim* to carry over their training in this matter to their *davening*.

The Rebbe's first great objective was to alter this mind-set and instill the radically different concept of granting full participation to the lips. The next problem the Rebbe tackled was that even those who did use their mouths in *davening* failed to enunciate all the words. The third issue involved the words that were said—many were not pronounced properly. The next issue was that the words that were read, frequently were not read correctly. So we can see that it was necessary for the Rebbe to make a major overhaul. The main breakthrough was to make clear a new concept: that the vocalizing of every sentence of every paragraph, every word of every sentence, and every syllable, letter, vowel, and accent of every word in the prayers we say has awesome significance and is necessary to complete spiritual circuits that have eternal, magnificent consequences.

All this was pertinent to the physical aspect of uttering the words. In addition to this, the *kehillah* had to be motivated to master the comprehension of the material and then to move on to mastering the art of *kavannah*.

- *Talk-Free Atmosphere*

A plague that overran shuls was the non-stop flow of talk during *davening*. Besides the fact that it was done during parts of the prayers when halachah explicitly prohibits it, it was terribly disrespectful. Eventually the situation deteriorated to the point where one could no longer hear any sound of the services over the loud voices of the rude congregants. The Rebbe eventually inculcated proper observance concerning this issue as well, making Rugby a model, talk-free synagogue.

The Rebbe was certainly successful in his overhaul on all these accounts. The sight of these *baalei batim davening* had no resemblance to the usual stereotype of this type of congregation. When the Rebbe's *baalei batim davened*, they resembled a first-class yeshivah at prayer.

- *Modesty Is the best Policy*

Perhaps we can say that the area of *tznius* presented the greatest challenge to the Rebbe. Inspiring the *kehillah* to be conscientious with regard to women's dress posed many difficulties. First is the halachic aspect; the whole concept that the Torah has dictates in this area— "kosher" and "nonkosher" garments—was shocking, and to some even unacceptable. Included in this were the strict dictates as to the parts of the body that may and may not be exposed. An important item very much neglected and misunderstood was the covering of the hair of a married woman. There was a tremendous leniency and general lack of observance of this halachah at that time in the United States among many religious groups, including wives of some noted *rabbanim*. The cause of this was difficult to understand, considering that the requirement for married women to cover their hair is stringent. But despite the opposition of the times, the Rebbe had a great influence in reversing this trend in his *kehillah*. Today, *baruch Hashem*, the picture has by and large changed and the general religious population adheres to proper observance of this requirement.

There are some aspects of modesty that are not subject to exact, clear, technical halachic guidelines, but rather stem from a general mentality and outlook—for example, the concept of making sure that the manner of dress is not alluring. This aspect of modesty reflects womankind's acceptance of the general responsibility of not presenting temptation to men and causing impure thoughts.

Attractive looks are actually a marvelous gift Hashem presented to woman for a very holy purpose. However, this gift must be guarded for this purpose only and therefore carries with it a great obligation. It places on all womankind a heavy responsibility of constantly being on guard. In conjunction with this thought, the Vilna Gaon states that this obligation and responsibility is the very reason the Torah exempted women from fulfilling commandments that bind them to a time frame, for they must have the freedom to keep their awareness constantly focused.

The issue of attractive clothing presents a particular difficulty since the fashions are always offering another new, eye-catching "look." One of the great women's clothing designers announced some years ago that his goal was to make every woman appear exceptionally attractive, whereas Jewish modesty dictates that a woman should aim to be inconspicuous.

Tznius also includes following the dictates of the Torah in all situations of interaction between men and women, from working in an office to having guests at the Shabbos table. Lighthearted intermingling was unheard of in the Rebbe's shul, and the *kehillah* adopted this Torah behavior in their personal lives as well.

- *The Gehinnom Waltz*

The Rebbe likewise enlightened his community on what is wrong with "mixed dancing," which many religious people engaged in at that time. He opened their eyes to the fact that this was something that, as religious Jews, they would never dream of doing on their own, yet because it was accepted as "social dancing" by the gentiles, it was condoned—which, of course, did not make any sense.

- *Inside Out*

The Rebbe brought attention to the fact that married women usually do not go out of their way to look especially nice for their husbands in the confines of the home. Yet, when going out of the house they made a special effort to look attractive. This results in a man thinking that his own wife is less attractive than the other women. He appealed to all to reverse this behavior.

- *What's in a Name?*

In those years almost all American Jews were given secular names at birth, which they thought of as their "real" names and used for all official purposes. The Hebrew name, which is technically the true name, was used on the rare occasion of being called up to the Torah. To give up these gentile names was a particularly difficult test since a name is one of the most personal, cherished possessions of any individual, for this is how he is known and referred to by all, the label that identifies him. The Rebbe, however, brought out in his campaign that many of these gentile names that they were so proud of and found so difficult to give up were actually the names of non-Jews responsible for wholesale bloodshed, torture, and suffering inflicted on our people over many centuries. It is important to keep in mind what *Chazal* told us, that retaining our Jewish names was a major contributing factor to our redemption from Egypt.

I have just shared a glimpse of the makings of the Rebbe's illustrious *kehillah* of today. These episodes are very precious and as time marches on the number of the living, privileged few who merited witnessing and being part of all this (they should all be well until 120) keeps dwindling.

Fortunate are those who were witness to this historical, unparalleled spiritual revolution.

With great difficulty I back away and take leave of this little, old but holy structure, and I anxiously await the fulfillment of *Chazal's* dictum that some day we will see it rebuilt in Yerushalayim.

CHAPTER THIRTY-THREE

Torah, Torah

This chapter in itself does not relate to a walk. It is, however, connected to the previous chapter, which is linked to a walk. As we mentioned there, the subject of Torah deserves its own place.

Previously we described the awesome growth and transition of the *baalei batim* into strong mitzvah observers. It was only in the area of Torah study that they remained stagnant. They literally had no serious Torah learning. Even if they attended a class or a lecture on occasion, this was not by any means Torah study, which involves having and exercising the ability to pick up a Torah text and actually read and understand it on one's own. Their lack of Torah education and proper background in their youth prevented this.

One Shabbos when the Rebbe rose to deliver his Shabbos *derashah*, he said, "My fondest dear ones, members of this, my beautiful *kehillah*, there are absolutely no words of praise great enough for you, for your grand scale metamorphosis. You have made such a great, meaningful changeover and movement to place yourselves under the wings of the *Shechinah*. You have acquired a true love and respect for *lomdei Torah*; you support Torah and yearn that your offspring should become *talmidei chachamim*. However, standing alongside a bookcase of holy books, you feel as though this is something foreign to you, something with which you have no connection. Every Jew must come to the next world with Torah. Torah, and only Torah, enables us to arise at *techiyas hameisim*. A Jew must be connected with the *Shas*, he must have a firm sense that it belongs to him. He must be able to point to the holy pages and say that they are his and he must know them well. The whole *Shas*, a part, a tractate, a chapter, a page, a line, or a word—this is *my* word, this is *my* portion in Torah. He must have a portion and know it."

After a positive response to this inspiring appeal the Rebbe embarked on organizing a serious learning program for the *baalei batim*. It was something so unique that it was probably the only one of its kind in existence at that time. The best terminology to describe this operation is a "Torah explosion." In the process of delivering a conventional layman's Torah lesson, the information is presented by reading the material to the students, resulting in different degrees of absorption by the usually confused, and often bored, listeners. The Rebbe created and activated an innovative, realistic, practical Torah learning program. To begin with he had electrical outlets installed at every seat in the shul. Not only did he grant permission for the *baalei batim* to record the lesson, but he insisted that they all do so and then use the recording to aid them in reviewing the material, which was understandably foreign to them. He then had them review the subject matter with one another and then tested them on the subject matter. That's a pretty serious program.

When the program began the pace was indeed very slow. First the *baalei batim* had to learn how to read the words correctly: the proper punctuation; the translation of each word; the sentence structure; all this leading to the crown, which was to get a clear picture of the logical sequence. After a full year the amount covered was perhaps one page! But the Rebbe's dream was beginning to be realized—they were now connected. They now possessed something with which to come to the next world. The Rebbe was about to conquer the last of the uncaptured territory.

The Rebbe went on to a completely new dimension, something which was never dreamed of for *baalei batim* of this caliber. The Rebbe actually motivated them to undertake learning to the point that they were able to recite the Talmudic discussion, the question-and-answer sequence, by heart. This is not an easy undertaking. Besides the difficulty in the actual memorization, the material must be crystal-clear. To top it all, the participants had to be prepared to demonstrate this accomplishment in front of the Rebbe! Can you imagine the scene? Mature adults, heads of families, accomplished in their fields—police sergeant, chemist, college professor—submitting themselves like little boys to be tested by the Rebbe. As time went on their accomplishments became more substantial, and finally, to the joyous surprise of all, they completed a whole chapter. There is something about the completion of a chapter that gives one a strong sense of accomplishment. Besides the psychological factor in this feeling, it seems obvious that *Chazal*, through their Divine inspiration, must have inserted into the material this intrinsic feeling of accomplishment. The joy the participants felt was ecstatic and spurred them on to strive for the accomplishment of one more *perek*. This inspiration bore fruit and they went on to the acquisition of *perek* after *perek*.

In honor of this great achievement, the Rebbe requested that a special banquet be arranged. At this gala affair, the *wives* of the participants were called to the dais and each woman was presented with a gift. This was to show recognition and admiration of the fact that this magnificent accomplishment would not have been possible without their noble cooperation and their demonstration that they valued the cause.

[A number of years after settling in *Eretz Yisrael* I received a phone call from one of the dear *baalei batim* (a chemist) of the Rugby community. He was in *Eretz Yisrael* for a visit, and asked if he could come to see me. When he arrived I observed that he was holding a small volume of the *Shas*. This is something one usually sees in the hand of a *ben Torah* of stature. After exchanging brief greetings and dispensing with the usual formalities and reminiscing, he explained that a chapter he had studied in Tractate *Kesubos* was becoming a little rusty in his mind. He then asked if I could review those areas which he felt were not clear to him. No touring itinerary was more important than clarifying a piece of *gemara*!]

Next, the Rebbe extended the perimeters of the program in a unique way. He instituted giving numerous *gemara* classes during the week. Instead of the usual way of teaching the same *perek* throughout the week, he did as follows: He offered a number of different chapters in various tractates on different days of the week, on a weekly basis. For example, Sunday night was the fourth chapter in *Sanhedrin*, Wednesday night the second chapter in *Bava Metzia*. For many of the *baalei batim*, a *shiur* once a week supplied ample material for the necessary work they had laid out for themselves from the first step until memorization. Others, who had advanced further, could choose to attend two or even three of the weekly *shiurim* on different chapters. This system also presented a variety of subject matter that could be chosen even for those who attended only once a week. In this way each layman was able to participate in the program according to his abilities.

The time frame of my walks with the Rebbe focused on the period when the shul was in East Flatbush, the birthplace of the *kehillah* and the scene of its development. Unfortunately the neighborhood was deteriorating, and the Rebbe eventually decided to uproot the *kehillah* and transplant the shul to Ocean Parkway in Flatbush. There, in the shul which was now called *Beis Yisrael*, the Rebbe expanded his Torah revolution to an even greater degree. He presented a number of these *gemara shiurim* in the morning hours, a time when most of the congregants were normally preoccupied with their various professions. The Rebbe inspired the participants to the extent that they managed to take time off from their busy schedules for a morning *shiur* on a *perek*, and sometimes more. Sunday was a day that was completely filled with learning, a full schedule devoted to these programs.

I am about to relate something so awesome and incredible that I hesitate, for fear that many will find it too far-fetched to believe. I already related that the *baalei batim* accomplished their learning laboriously at first, starting with one page. One by one, these pages finally added up to a *perek*, and these chapters eventually added up to a tractate. Can you imagine a layman being tested on the question-and-answer sequence of a whole tractate? After years of study, the tractates added up, one after another. With the passing of many years that ultimate of accomplishments came to reality; some of the *baalei batim* in the program actually completed the entire *Shas* with the Rebbe.

How fortunate it was to be a layman with the Rebbe—the entire *Shas*!

Torah, Torah …

CHAPTER THIRTY-FOUR

The Short Walk

I walked into shul a little late one Shabbos morning and was in for a big surprise, greater than I ever would have expected. The Rebbe was at his place in front but instead of his usual position, facing *mizrach*, he was facing the *kehillah*. As soon as he saw me walk in, he dramatically walked to the back, and with all eyes on him he came right over to me. Imagine how I felt, realizing that I had prevented the Rebbe from commencing his prayers since he had patiently waited for me to appear. I do not remember this ever happening before or after this incident. He then requested that I step outside with him. This indeed was becoming more and more suspenseful. We walked outside together, and this was certainly our shortest walk. Once outside the shul the Rebbe said to me: "Will you accept the position of music director of the Rugby youth program?"

In my early youth I had studied music. The Rebbe was aware of this; however, he never made mention of it or made any reference to it, or even reflected having paid any attention to this fact. My shock was total—now music director?! My amazement was broken by the Rebbe again addressing me. "Don't let this burden you, for it won't come to actuality." He then led me back inside, returned to his place in front, and was then able to commence *davening*. What was this "director" business all about?

Our most powerful leaders and *rabbanim*, charismatic and eloquent speakers, were successful in influencing the masses. However, there were always individuals who were not moved or influenced, and to various degrees some were opponents or even vicious antagonists of these *manhigim*. Rav Hutner explained the *Chazal* stating that Mashiach will have many names. These names symbolize that only he will have a synthesis of personality traits and qualities that will capture and captivate everyone. Until then, even the greatest among us will be harassed and obstructed by adversaries.

Despite the spectacular success the Rebbe enjoyed, he also had his share of individuals who resisted his inspiration and even presented opposition at times. One group of these opponents raised the issue of youth groups, which were non-existent in Rugby, and were an integral part of the Young Israel movement and most Modern Orthodox synagogues. Unfortunately, youth activities in many places were run in a manner that was not in accordance with halachah or the spirit of Torah. In addition, the financial burden of running these groups was heavy. They required housing, equipment, and above all a large, capable staff of experts in various fields. The budget for all this was customarily met by having the adult congregants organize committees that arranged assorted fundraising activities: bazaars, bingo, and other entertainment. These events themselves were a major social activity for the congregants, not necessarily run in the spirit of Torah, often featuring improper levity and immodest mingling of men and women.

The war cry of the renegades was: "Who ever heard of a Young Israel without a youth center?" For the congregants to get involved with all the usual membership meetings and social activities that were required for establishing a youth center would be contrary to the Torah behavior that the Rebbe was carefully instilling in them. Besides, the Rebbe was channeling all efforts to motivate them to devote their free time to attending the Torah classes.

All this was supposedly for the youngsters—for the youth! What youth? Most of the offspring of the *kehillah* were already enrolled in top Torah institutions. They certainly were not youth center clientele, whereas the neighborhood youth were in no way interested in what the Rugby Young Israel had to offer. Nevertheless these stubborn opponents insisted on raising the youth department storm. The Rebbe saw through all this and understood that it was just the glamour of the weekly fundraising meetings and activities that actually motivated them. As absurd as it was, the rebels were successful in creating enough waves over the issue that a wound had been opened and had to be healed. An important criterion for the Rebbe's continued success with the *kehillah* was the high esteem in which they held him. Now these opponents succeeded in fostering an opinion that it was wrong not to have youth activities—and that perhaps the Rebbe was guilty of not fulfilling his responsibilities. This jeopardized the Rebbe's influence on the *kehillah*. It could not be ignored, and the rebels could not just be put down. How would the Rebbe handle this one?

There was always an aura of mystery surrounding the Rebbe's Shabbos morning *derashos*. We never knew if he would go up to speak until he actually stepped up. There were absolutely no rules or guidelines. The anxious anticipation for me and many others was immeasurable. By far these *derashos* were the high point of the week. Shabbos after Shabbos, I sat staring at the Rebbe. Would he go up or not? I was able to feel my heart pounding from anxiety. At times he would go up and to my great disappointment just make a few routine announcements, wishing some *mazel tovs*, giving updates on the learning schedule, etc., and then return to his place.

Then one Shabbos before Mussaf the Rebbe rises. I am waiting anxiously. The Rebbe makes some announcements, the *mazel tovs*, the schedule. Is he closing? No—he is continuing, wonderful. Expecting an inspiring *derashah*, I hear the following: "I am proud to announce the grand opening of the new gala youth program of the Rugby Young Israel." What followed was probably one of the most brilliant acts of diplomacy ever witnessed.

There was a close circle of people who were especially devoted to the Rebbe. Many of these people, some of whom had by now become *talmidei chachamim*, had in their youth excelled in diversified fields. The Rebbe, with his ingenious mind and memory, put this information to magnificent use. One was a talented general youth leader who had served as a successful head counselor and camp director; one was a general sports director; another was an expert baseball coach; another excelled in basketball; yet another in tennis and another in soccer. Then there was the expert in arts and crafts; the great specialist in drama and plays; and there was little old me and my music. The Rebbe then proceeded, of course with permission from all of us, to present the most sparkling youth program anyone could desire. Going down the list he described each field of activity, together with the name of the director of each department. As the Rebbe announced the name of each appointee, he added a brief, complimentary resume of his past positions and talents. Upon completing, the Rebbe then explained that all this would be conducted and run by the talented, famous youth director, and then mentioned by name our friend who had this talent.

What the Rebbe had miraculously done was to put together a superb youth program without the fanfare, the levity, the immodest meetings; without the fat cigars (they were always a "must" at these gatherings); without the bazaars, bingo and big, time-wasting fundraising campaigns; without the brotherhood and sisterhood.

"Our youth department is ready to go into action and start immediately. We are just waiting for you, my dear congregants, to bring in the youth." This, *baruch Hashem*, was the last that was heard of the matter.

CHAPTER THIRTY-FIVE

The Rebbe, the Mechanech

*I*t was customary when one became engaged that one made the rounds of the *rabbanim*, seeking their advice and special guidance. Each one has his prepared little speech, his time-honored advice and guidelines for happiness. I was now a *chasan* and contemplating putting in my request to the Rebbe that he share his advice on that day's walk. The reason for my hesitation is not difficult to fathom. I could make the rounds of all the *rabbanim*, but in the case of the Rebbe I had been receiving input for years and years, all of which was related in some way to good marriage advice. How could I possibly say to the Rebbe: What is your advice on preparation for marriage?

Finally, I posed the question anyway and was very pleased that I did. The Rebbe compiled a personalized marriage training program for me. I incorporated this program into my book *Don't Judge a Book by Its Cover*, a guide to finding one's mate, one of the few books to which the Rebbe ever gave a *haskamah*. I devoted one chapter to preparing for marriage, offering advice on how a person can elevate his capacity to be a good marriage partner. I present here the program that the Rebbe presented to me, for your benefit:

Exercise #1:

Pick an individual you know, and spend a few minutes each day thinking about how you can contribute to their happiness. Even if this person has "everything" in the world, there still may be something you can do to make them happy. When you first start doing this exercise, your mind may draw a blank. What could you possibly do for them? But as you focus on the person's character and needs, ideas will come to you slowly but surely. This is a great accomplishment. When you strain your mind to find something you can do to make another individual happy, you are generating a tremendous, positive effect on your own soul, and developing your potential to be a kind and generous person.

Exercise #2:

Pick someone you know and think of how you can help them. What is the difference between this and the first exercise, since by helping someone you will certainly make him happy? The difference is that in Exercise #1 the person may not have a care, worry, or problem. Nevertheless we can make him happy. In Exercise #2 we focus on a definite problem they have—something lacking, something difficult, some cause of anguish which we attempt to resolve. For example, you may know an older *bachur* who needs help in finding a *shidduch*. True, the first thing that might come to your mind is, "Who am I? I'm not a *shadchan*; I don't know people; I don't know any single girls; I have no contacts. How can I help this person? I'd love to help him, but what can I do?" But, the truth is, if you really exert yourself, and think as hard as you can, an idea may occur to you. Perhaps you have an aunt in Bnei Brak who has contacts. And if she doesn't know anybody, maybe she has a friend, or a friend's friend, who might know of somebody suitable. At first, you couldn't come up with anything to help this *bachur*. But by perservering, these thoughts came into your head. This, too, has a great effect on developing our "*chesed* muscles."

- *Exercise #3:*

It is very important to develop an appreciation of the good qualities of your prospective mate. One way to do this is by writing down six positive attributes that this person has. This can also be done by simply thinking about this person and picturing all their good character traits. This, too, is a great exercise in developing a positive outlook and loving feelings toward people.

I would like to present two other valuable exercises from the Rebbe, also from Chapter 8 of my book. Although it is not mentioned there, all the exercises in that chapter are from the Rebbe.

- *Smiling*

Another suggestion, from *gedolim*, is to train yourself to smile at people throughout the course of the day. But this can be difficult even if you are a natural smiler, because a smile is like the weather —it can blow this way or that. If you are in a good mood, you smile; if not, then you don't smile. We have to train ourselves to smile even if we are in a bad mood. It may be false. It may not be natural. Imagine that your best friend is getting married, and you happen to be in a terrible mood on the day of the wedding. Are you going to drag yourself around at the wedding with a depressed look on your face? Probably not. You will force yourself to put on an act. You'll dance and sing with a happy expression on your face, for the sake of your friend. It may be false, but you have to do it nevertheless. The same thing applies to a smile. Though they don't always come from the heart, our facial expressions still give off signals and have a tremendous impact on people around us.

This is especially true in marriage. A young man comes home after a hard day in the yeshivah, tired, and perhaps disappointed because he worked so hard on understanding the *gemara* but not everything was clear to him. On the other side of the door, his wife is eagerly looking forward to seeing him. If he comes home depressed, with a sour expression on his face, he will cause his wife great anguish. He must train himself to be conscious of his facial expressions, and to enter the house with a cheerful countenance. That is his *avodas Hashem* at this minute. By making himself cheerful and upbeat when he enters his home, he will put a positive spin on the entire evening. The collective effect of those few moments each day on one's marriage is crucial, and goes a long way toward setting the standard for peace and happiness in one's home.

Rabbi Moshe Shimon Weintraub *zt"l*, one of the giants of our generation, relatively not so well known, quoting a Chassidic source, said that even a false smile is imbued with holiness. The *Chumash* says that when Yaakov Avinu decided to leave the house of Lavan, he told his wives: "Your father's face is not toward me as before" (*Bereishis* 31:5). What he meant was, "Your father Lavan no longer smiles at me, so it is time for me to leave." But how did Yaakov Avinu know that Lavan's facial expression meant that he should depart?

We know from Kabbalistic teachings that there were sparks of holiness captured by Lavan which were trapped on the "side of impurity." Yaakov was trying to redeem these sparks of holiness. In order for a person to produce a smile—even a false smile— *kedushah* has to be present. When Yaakov Avinu saw that Lavan's face had changed, and that Lavan couldn't produce even a fake smile, he knew that he had taken out every spark of holiness that was there, and that he had finished his job and it was time to leave.

The exercise here consists of smiling at people during the course of the day. It shouldn't be done in an exaggerated, silly way. Just be aware of your facial expression, and try to smile. It is known that many *gedolim* practiced smiling. Rabbi Yisrael Salanter would practice in front of a mirror. He wanted to perfect a smile that was appealing and that would make another person feel good.

- *Anticipating*

The ability to see what is coming is an important trait in overcoming many of life's trials, especially in the area of marriage. As the mishnah in *Pirkei Avos* says, "Who can we consider as wise, one who can anticipate the development and outcome of a situation." Think about all the possible problems that might arise in a new situation, and prepare yourself for them.

Usually, there are two types of challenges that we encounter: unexpected difficulties (which we can prepare for by constantly maintaining a high level of awareness and fear of Hashem), and the more prevalent challenges that are usually predictable, either because of our past experiences or through logical deduction projected into the future. For example, if you have to deal with an individual who consistently loses his temper under stress—which in turn brings out the worst in you, and leads to a chain reaction of hurtful and negative responses—the best thing for you to do is to avoid the whole situation by anticipating the attack and acting accordingly. By seeing what may come, all the heartache and pain can be avoided.

A husband returns home at the end of a day. He has had a wonderful day in the yeshivah, or at his office, and is in a good mood. His wife, however, has had a terrible day. The washing machine broke down, the oven stopped working in the middle of preparing supper, and she faced numerous difficulties and disappointments throughout the course of the day. By evening, she feels like a wreck. The husband walks into the house and his wife makes antagonistic remarks to him. He answers her, and before you know it, they are quarreling. What this husband should have said to himself before walking into the house is, "It's possible I will find my wife in a terrific mood, or she may be very angry with me because she had a bad day. This happens sometimes. I understand that it's not her fault. If it happens, I'm not going to answer back. I'll try to be understanding." If a person would just spend a few seconds of preparation before walking into the house, the chances of his standing up to a test would be much greater. And while there is not any guarantee that he won't lose his temper or get annoyed, he will have a much easier time exercising self-control if he prepares himself in advance.

This whole concept of a program of exercises is one of the Rebbe's unique developments. It is important to understand that the entire process of training oneself for a positive trait has really been practiced by *Klal Yisrael*—men and women—since the giving of the Torah at Mt. Sinai, and even prior to this, starting from our Patriarchs and probably before. Today, however, the generally accepted concept is that when one is inspired by something he has heard or read concerning a person who has made achievements in Hashem's service— such as developing a certain character trait or diligence in one's Torah studies—this inspiration is sufficient to spur him on to the acquisition of the trait. This notion, however, is a great fallacy. The work only *begins* after one is inspired by reading or hearing a talk about a desirable trait. This should then lead a person *to take action* to make a real acquisition of the trait.

In order to achieve such a goal, a concrete, practical system must be implemented. This entails adopting what we can call a spiritual exercise. The Vilna Gaon tells us that we must be enlightened in our service of Hashem by observing what we find in the "world." This might be one of the meanings intended by *Chazal* when they said, "*Derech eretz kadma laTorah* — [Understanding] the ways of the world is a prerequisite to fulfilling the Torah." If a person wants to become adept at any field in the world, besides engaging himself in the intellectual pursuit and the theoretical aspects, it is imperative to program it into his very being. This holds true with everything from medicine to the arts. The integration into our system is done through training, and this likewise applies to Torah.

Because of the Rebbe's desire to see in his *talmidim* realistic, concrete accomplishments, he was not satisfied with delivering his powerful, beautiful talks. With his great insight, practicality, and creativity the Rebbe put together training programs to effect tangible accomplishment. He presented them in *shiurim* and to individuals who sought his advice, as in my case. They took their most aggressive form in the Rebbe's *vaadim*.

A *vaad* was made up of six to eight members who had in common their marital status, age, and the type of yeshivah they attended. Some groups met on a weekly basis and others biweekly. One of the most important elements of the system was secrecy. Nothing about it was allowed to be revealed, especially what took place at the meetings. The Rebbe had a complete network of many such groups covering a broad spectrum of yeshivah types, and no group knew that another existed. I had knowledge of them since I had the *zechus* of assisting the Rebbe to organize them. My involvement was from approximately 1959 until 1965, at which point I moved to *Eretz Yisrael*.

To take a peek into the *vaad* itself: Each meeting was short and intense, taking about 20 minutes. The Rebbe would give a brief discourse on a specific subject and then present the exercise of the week. The session always began with an account, given by each member, of his undertakings during the preceding week, followed by the Rebbe's comments on the members' feedback. There was a certain period when the members of the group that met biweekly had to mail their weekly report to the Rebbe on a postcard. The broad spectrum of traits that were worked on included various areas of service between man and his Creator and between man and his fellow.

After living in *Eretz Yisrael* for a number of years, I eventually got up enough courage to ask the Rebbe if I could set up a *vaad* in *Eretz Yisrael* according to all his specifications and following the established procedure, with the Rebbe's input supplied by him in the form of a recording. After much effort on my part, the Rebbe eventually agreed to provide the tapes, but only including the "short talk," introducing and explaining the issue of the week. The "exercise of the week" we would have to create for ourselves.

(Once I received a call from a stranger regarding the Rebbe's *vaad*. He had asked the Rebbe a question and the Rebbe had replied that he should consult with me, as I was the "expert" on his *vaadim*.)

Eventually, when the right conditions presented themselves, I finally began conducting *vaadim*, attempting to cling to the Rebbe's system, which I have continued doing, *be'ezras Hashem*, to this day. I have seen in the course of the years quite positive results.

At the famous Thursday night lectures the Rebbe eventually presented his unique program of growth exercises to the public—The Ten Steps to Greatness (tape #706)—which I would like to present here.

1. Spend at least 30 seconds each day thinking about THE WORLD TO COME — *Olam Haba*.

   Ponder that we are in this world only as a preparation for the World to Come. This is the purpose of life.

2. Spend a few private seconds each day and say to Hashem, "I LOVE YOU, HASHEM."

   You will be fulfilling a positive commandment from the Torah. This will kindle a fire in your heart and will have a powerful effect on your character. Your exterior bestirs your interior.

3. Every day do one act of kindness that no one knows about, in secrecy. Have intention beforehand that you are doing this in order to fulfill your program to achieve greatness.

   The practice of doing acts of kindness—*GEMILUS CHASADIM*—is one of the three most important functions in the world.

   Examples
   - If you are the first one in the *beis midrash*, put the books in their proper order and place. If your wife is not in the kitchen, clean a few dishes or straighten up for her without her knowing.
   - If you should see something potentially dangerous on the sidewalk, clear it off to the side so no one will be harmed.

4. Encourage someone every day. "HASHEM ENCOURAGES THE HUMBLE." Have in mind that you are doing it because of "The Program." Anonymous letters of kindness can do a great deal of good to encourage people.

5. Spend one minute every day thinking about what happened yesterday.

   "Let us search out our ways and investigate."

   Everyone should have his mind on what he is doing—by reviewing yesterday's actions daily.

6. Make all your actions for the purpose of Heaven. Say it once a day.

   Example
   - "I am doing this in order to be more aware of Hashem."

7. Be aware of the principle, "Man was created in the image of Hashem."

   Every human face is a reflection of Hashem. Your face is like a screen and your soul like a projector which projects onto your face the glory of the human soul, which has in it the greatness of Hashem.

   Once a day, picture a face, any face, and think, "I am seeing the image of Hashem." You will begin to understand the endless nobility of a face.

8. Once a day give a person a full smile.

   Just as Hashem shines on us, we should smile on others.

   Smile because Hashem wants you to, even if you really do not feel like it.

   When you smile, have intention that you are doing it for the purpose of coming closer to Hashem through the Ten Steps to Greatness.

9. "Hashem clothes the naked."

   Clothing is a testament to the nobility of man. Man is unique—he has free will, has a soul made in the image of Hashem. Even Angels are beneath Man in greatness. To demonstrate the superiority of mankind we must be clothed.

   Spend 30 seconds in the morning thinking about our garments: what a gift they are from Hashem. Say *MALBISH ARUMIM*" (He clothes the naked) out loud.

10. Spend time each day thinking about Yerushalayim during the time of the Temple. Every day, sit on the floor before going to sleep. Spend one second on the floor, and mourn for the destruction of Yerushalayim. Think: "If I should forget you, Yerushalayim, let my right arm forget its cunning."

    "The wise man seizes the opportunity to do mitzvos" (*Mishlei* 10:8). The lazy person says, someday I'll do it.

If you start this program, after thirty days you will be tired. So wait six months until you start again. Do another thirty days, then wait five months, and so on. After a while you might do it all the time. If you do it even for one day, you are extraordinary.

Thank you, Rebbe, thank you.

CHAPTER THIRTY-SIX

Beware! Feelings Are Everywhere

On one walk I remember well, the Rebbe discussed a life-or-death issue. The subject matter might be a little heavy for our framework here, but because of its vital importance, I wish to share it. It is a subject we must always be mindful of, but especially so in our times. We are living in a generation that particularly needs strengthening in the matter of sensitivity to the feelings of others. We must generate an awareness of the necessity for caution in our communication, so as not to hurt or degrade others.

The year is sometime in the late 1950's. The location is a state institution for the mentally ill. The characters are a group of patients occupying a common ward. The episode is a catastrophe: a supposedly non-aggressive inmate suddenly attacks a fellow patient. The poor, innocent victim is beaten until life is snuffed out of his body. The ramifications and significance extend far beyond the simple horror of the incident.

As we walked, the Rebbe spoke about a young man to whom he had been close. He was a sincere *bachur,* a *yirei Shamayim* with a fine character. He was of average intelligence, but he had a strong will power that could have driven him to greatness far beyond that which many more brilliant young men achieve. There was nothing unusual or outstanding about him; perhaps he was a little more sensitive than most to negative remarks or actions. The Rebbe had a warm, close relationship with this *bachur* and had hopes for a bright future for him. After not seeing the boy for a while, the Rebbe made inquiries that led him to the following revelation: Without warning or provocation the young man had been accosted with a sudden barrage of nasty insults and harassment. Not expecting this, he was caught off-guard and took it very much to heart—too much. The trauma of the incident was so great that it left him in a state of emotional shock that spiraled into a severe nervous breakdown necessitating hospitalization.

Upon hearing this, the Rebbe immediately rushed to the mental institution to visit the boy, hoping that their close relationship would allow his comforting words to penetrate and perhaps help the boy to "snap back." The Rebbe described how he was allowed to sit and speak with him, and the devastating disappointment that followed. He spoke warmly, trying to rekindle their close relationship, but the boy just sat staring glassy-eyed into space, not even noticing his visitor. The Rebbe made several trips, each time failing to evoke even the slightest acknowledgment of his presence. And then, one day, the Rebbe heard the horrible news of the murder of this young yeshivah man in the ward.

The Rebbe expounded on the extreme caution one must exercise in all communications, and the realization we must have of the awesome responsibility for the repercussions our words can cause. This is echoed in the words of *Chazal* in the Midrash on *Parashas Chukas*, When Rabbi Shimon ben Gamliel requested that his servant purchase the choicest cut of meat, and on another occasion, the least desirable cut, he received the tongue both times. *Chazal* explain that there is no enjoyment, thrill, or pleasure greater than that afforded by the tongue, meaning that through the power of speech one can actually cause the greatest joy to another; and conversely, the opposite is likewise true, that through the power of speech one can cause the greatest pain and anguish.

We can all attest to the truth of this when we are the victims, the recipients of unkind, hurtful communication from others. We could compose complete volumes on our unfortunate, unpleasant experiences. I would like to share, however, the following episode for its powerful message, similar to that of the Rebbe's story, as heard from our very capable and dedicated editor, Mrs. Lavon.

After surviving the Holocaust, a young woman made her way from Europe to *Eretz Yisrael*, where she found a job teaching in a prestigious *frum* high school. Because of the difficulty of finding a suitable *shidduch* in the wake of the Holocaust, she had remained single.

She was very dedicated to her job, always on time for work without fail, and was popular with the students. However, after a number of years of teaching, she had a class that did not appreciate her. One day the girls decided to cause trouble as an expression of their displeasure. Their plan was to go on strike, refusing to respond to her in any way. When she came into class the next day and asked them to open their *Chumashim*, they ignored her. She repeated her request, but they just sat there. After failing to evoke any response from them, she told them that obviously there was a problem in this class, and that she wanted each of them to write down honestly what she thought the problem was and hand the paper in to her. The girls did so, each one writing as she saw fit. The teacher then collected the papers and read them on the spot. As she read through them, she came to one that bluntly informed her that the writer did not like her because she was an "old maid." This insult upset the teacher so much that she took her handbag and rushed out of the classroom to her home, not telling anyone what had happened or where she was going.

The next day she did not appear, nor the next day. Nor did she get in touch with the school or send any message. This struck the school staff as very odd, since she had always been so dedicated and reliable. Finally, the principal decided to go to the teacher's home to find out what was wrong. When no one answered her knock, the principal entered the teacher's apartment and found her lifeless body there. She called the police; the coroner determined that she had died of a heart attack several days earlier . (The epilogue was that the girl who wrote the "killer" note was still not married or engaged as of the time the story was passed along, a number of years after the incident.)

The Rebbe stressed how much one must bear in mind the fact that one word can actually lead to the brutal, tragic removal of a precious, beautiful diamond of a *neshamah* from this world, with a whole life and future unfulfilled. The worst manifestation of this is when we are not even aware that we are causing hurt or to what extent. The positive side to keep in mind is how much happiness and joy we can bring to another human being. General advice on how to avoid hurting others is to cry out to Hashem in prayer, begging for Divine assistance so as not to cause the slightest anguish to another. The Rebbe gave us an eye-opening exercise to train us to get a clearer vision and achieve greater awareness in our communication: Take a few minutes each day to review all the communications you can recall from the previous day. Like an outsider watching a video, observe the day unfolding before you. The new insights and awareness that come from this exercise are amazing and very rewarding. For one who is striving to avoid acting with inconsideration to others, each find is a treasure.

CHAPTER THIRTY-SEVEN

It's About Rights and Wrongs

Yaakov Avinu, under the directive and strict orders of his mother Rivkah, a worthy prophetess, is commanded to engage in a perilous, life-threatening mission: he has the awesome responsibility of intercepting and obtaining the infinitely significant blessings of his father Yitzchak, to circumvent his bestowing them on Yaakov's wicked and powerful brother, Esav. Yaakov Avinu has absolutely no personal interest in this dangerous mission. He is performing this task solely because of the instructions he received from his prophetic mother for the sake of the future existence of *Klal Yisrael*. He is so frightened, and rightfully so, that angels have to support him and keep him standing upright.

The mission is a success, and Yaakov Avinu secures the *berachos*. When Esav discovers what had transpired and is struck by the realization of his inconceivable loss, in his great anger, disappointment, and frustration he emits an awesome, blood-curdling cry. It is a shocking revelation that Esav *HaRasha* possesses such a pure faith in the power of the simple words of a blessing.

Chazal (*Masechta Megillah* and *Midrash Rabbah*) pose a most surprising question: "When did Yaakov Avinu pay for the great anguish he caused his brother Esav?" They go on to explain that it was at the time of the terrifying Purim ordeal. Through this striking *Chazal*, the Rebbe opened a completely new dimension to us and gave us a fresh insight into the subject of sensitivity toward people's feelings. To tamper with Esav and hurt his feelings was the last thing in the world that Yaakov Avinu would ever want to do. Yaakov performed this heroic act only in obedience to his mother, for the sake of Hashem and *Klal Yisrael*. Yet, he is held responsible for the hurt feelings of his brother: "When did Yaakov pay for the hurt and anguish he caused Esav?" ... Indeed, an entirely new dimension.

In the course of our dealings with people, at times we feel the need to say a harsh word and express something that can sting. Often this is followed by pangs of guilt or doubt and we then attempt to review the episode, to reevaluate our actions to see if they were indeed justified and called for. We are obviously partial and can easily err. However, at times we are accurate in judging that we were *right* about the issue itself that called for our action, with its inevitable hurtful results. *"When did Yaakov Avinu pay for the anguish he caused Esav ..."* Even if our actions were unquestionably justified and on the mark, the anguish and pain we cause is taken so seriously by the Heavenly Tribunal that it sets into motion consequences stemming from the *middas hadin*—strict, harsh judgment which we cannot in any way escape.

I am not making an attempt here to explain or analyze the Rebbe's point. The concept itself obviously needs a lot of clarification in order to be understood. Nevertheless it is a reality and must be related to in that way.

The Rebbe then spoke about Rachel Imeinu, who, in an attempt to protect her father from the abomination of idol worship, confiscated his idols, which was surely a righteous act. However, because of the anguish she caused him, she did not escape punishment from the Heavenly Tribunal. I heard a very similar insight in the name of R' Chaim Shmulevitz *zt"l* and also (*l'havdil bein chaim l'chaim*) from HaRav Chaim Pinchas Scheinberg *shlita*.

To help put our subject into perspective, we can say that there are five basic categories of these anguish-causing situations, all of which carry an inevitable penalty:

1. One does not realize that he is hurting another.
2. One does not realize the extent of the hurt he is causing.
3. One hurts intentionally and does not care if he is wrong, rationalizing that a person has a right to lose his patience sometimes.
4. One realizes that he has hurt someone and has the mind-set to reconsider; he concludes that he was right, but in actuality he was wrong.
5. One thinks it over and concludes that he was right, and actually was right.

What an awesome concept! Even when justified, we can be punished; imagine the consequences when we are really wrong.

In *I Shmuel,* we find that Peninah taunted Chanah in order to give her an extra motivation for prayer so that she would be blessed with a child. Peninah had the most sacred and pure intentions—and her scheme was a grand success. Yet she was severely punished for the anguish she caused.

I knew a young man attending an American yeshivah who was brilliant, a *lamdan* of fine character and charming personality, good-looking, with leadership qualities, and from a comfortable family. When the time for a *shidduch* would come, I was sure he would be "snatched up" quickly. This young man became annoyed with a staff member of his yeshivah and set into motion a process that eventually caused the Rav to leave, hurt and dejected. It never occurred to the *bachur* to ask forgiveness for the havoc and devastation he had created in this man's life, for he was RIGHT. *Shidduch* time arrived for him. The seasons came and went and so did the years, and he did not find his mate. He emphatically rejected my prodding to ask forgiveness from that Rav. He cast off all my attempts to enlighten him with the Rebbe's insight regarding hurting others—about being wrong even if you are right. Eventually, as an older *bachur*, he was appointed to a position in a yeshivah. He was broken by his bachelorhood and ultimately he contracted a difficult illness and sometime later was forced to leave his position.

After a lengthy period of time I met him. He was with a woman, whom he introduced as his wife, and he proceeded to recount the following amazing chain of events. Some months before, he found himself traveling on the wrong bus. About to get off the bus, he found himself face to face—for the first time after all these years—with that Rav, his victim. All at once he realized that this was *hashgachah pratis* and he recalled the words of the Rebbe that I had tried time and again to impress upon him. On the spot, he engaged the Rav in conversation, earnestly asking him for *mechilah*. Almost immediately after this incident the young man found his *zivug* and was finally happily married.

I have seen over and over again severe punishment inflicted for causing anguish to others. If one is guilty on this account, even for so-called "good reasons," it is imperative that he achieve a full, heartfelt forgiveness from his victim.

The Rebbe stressed to us that when asking *mechilah* one should really ask for forgiveness and plead one's cause, not just parrot the words. For example, he should explain that he acted the way he did due to the inordinate stress he was under and that afterwards he felt terrible that he had lost control of himself and caused anguish. The victim should not feel pressured or intimidated into forgiving; he should really feel that he has found it in his heart to forgive. One must also rectify the hurtful statements he made. For example, if in his anger he said, "No wonder nobody likes you," then when asking *mechilah* he must not just ask to be forgiven for his anger, but must also deal with the issue he raised of the victim not being liked. In the heat of his anger, he presented this remark as a fact, and the impression it left will continue to cause anguish until it is erased. It is imperative, therefore, that he get across the message that the statement had no basis in truth, but was fabricated in his anger.

If the victim does not forgive when asked, one must try again at another time. Asking *mechilah* should not be just a mechanical repetition of empty words, repeated three times. Rather, before asking again, one should put in a lot of serious thought as to a new angle of approach that will appeal to the victim's sympathy and arouse his willingness to forgive.

Even when you're right, you're wrong —
and when you're wrong, that's right.

Thank you, Rebbe, for opening our eyes to this most vital and important matter.

CHAPTER THIRTY-EIGHT

The Holy Shoebox

While sitting in his small, modest corner, the Rebbe exerted his influence on thousands around the globe through the books he published and the tapes of his *shiurim*. In his writings, his subjects included a general, all-encompassing Torah ideology, history, prayer, and *Chumash*. Three books were devoted to ideology: *Rejoice, O Youth*; *Sing, You Righteous*; and *Awake, My Glory*. Two books, *Behold a People* and *Torah Nation*, dealt with Jewish history. On prayer he wrote *Praise, My Soul*. His *sefarim* on *Chumash* include: *The Beginning*, on *Bereishis*; *A Nation Is Born*, on *Shemos*; *A Kingdom of Kohanim*, on *Vayikra*; *Journey Into Greatness*, on *Bamidbar*; and the last, which was published shortly before the Rebbe's *petirah*, *Fortunate Nation*, on *Devarim*.

When the Rebbe shared his plans for publishing his first book, *Rejoice, O Youth*, it afforded those of us who were close to him a tremendous feeling of joy. We appreciated so much all that we had gained from him that we yearned to see this great light go forth and shine upon the world.

My younger sister Naomi had the *zechus* of typing his first handwritten manuscript to prepare it for the publisher; I suspect she was deemed worthy of this for the many years that she had consistently attended the Rebbe's *shiurim*, very often being the only one in the *ezras nashim*. I would like to share some interesting and valuable background information regarding *Praise, My Soul*, the Rebbe's volume on *tefillah*.

There is an important tool, a helpful approach the Rebbe gave us, that can be applied to almost anything one studies. Concerning *Mesillas Yesharim*, the Rebbe explained that although its author, Rabbi Moshe Chaim Luzatto (Ramchal), declared in his introduction that this *sefer* contained very few new insights, it was actually full of precious gems which, if properly studied, would be found to be meaningful *chiddushim*. The commentary that the Rebbe suggested using to reveal these *chiddushim* was the "Rosh." This statement stunned all those present since Rabbeinu Asher, the *Rishon* who was popularly referred to as the Rosh, had lived hundreds of years prior to the Ramchal. The Rebbe then surprised us all by explaining that by the "Rosh," he meant our own individual thinking faculties.

It is important to take note that the conventional system used when delving into the depth of a subject is to immediately engage the commentaries. The Rebbe, however, explained that one's own "Rosh" is one of the most precious, insightful, and rich commentaries we have available. Although this idea is simple and obvious, somehow this limitless source of treasures is often overlooked. We must train ourselves to make use of it. Becoming accustomed to using this system takes patience, perseverance, imagination, creativity, ingenuity and originality. The Rebbe really opened our minds to the opportunity before us to make practical use of this power. He guided us by presenting an exercise of reading a few lines of *Mesillas Yesharim* daily, and not continuing further until our "Rosh" led to us discover at least one *chiddush*. Subsequently, he extended the exercise to other areas in Torah.

There was another major subject in which the Rebbe opened the doors to new avenues of thought and insight with his "*perush haRosh*," and that was in prayer. He explained that we invest considerable energy and thought in striving to understand the commentaries of the *Achronim* on the *gemara*; even more so when we delve into the commentaries of the *Rishonim;* and even more when we seek to interpret the *gemara* and *Mishnayos* themselves. How much more mental effort, then, should be invested in Torah that comes from before this era! Just think—the *Shemoneh Esrei* was composed by the *Anshei Knesses HaGedolah*! And what can be said concerning *pesukei d'zimrah* and other parts of *davening* that quote from the *Tehillim* of David HaMelech?

I heard the Rebbe address this subject in numerous *shiurim* and *vaadim*. On a walk I remember well, the Rzebbe provided me with a private discussion on this valuable subject of the "Rosh," revolving it around *tefillah*. He suggested that whenever I was blessed with a new insight in *davening*, I should write each thought on an index card, adding that he himself made a practice of this.

When we arrived at his home, the Rebbe invited me upstairs. There he beckoned me to come into his private room. He took out a shoebox and opened it, and I was amazed to see that it was packed with index cards, which the Rebbe lovingly caressed. Each one contained a single thought, a new insight on *tefillah*. The Rebbe remarked that if one does this consistently, he might gather enough material to publish a book.

The Rebbe then said to me that maybe, some day, he would publish these insights—*Praise, My Soul*.

Praise the Rebbe's soul!

CHAPTER THIRTY-NINE

The Silent Walk

A s previously mentioned, in the framework of his Thursday night lecture series, the Rebbe gave a speech which he called "The Ten Steps to Greatness" (tape # 706). Subsequently, a synopsis of this was published. The Rebbe wrote something there which has always puzzled me. The tenth item says as follows: "Spend time each day thinking about Yerushalayim during the time of the Temple. Every day, sit on the floor (before going to sleep); spend one second on the floor, and mourn for the destruction of Yerushalayim. Think, 'If I should forget you, Yerushalayim, let my right arm forget it's cunning.'" For years I have wondered: What could possibly be the significance, purpose, or reason for spending *one second* on the floor?

My own personal guess is as follows: People in our generation generally have difficulty relating to the *churban*, despite the fact that everyone agrees in theory about the importance of this matter. One of the major causes of this difficulty in relating is that people just do not seem to get around to it; they are too busy with other important things. The Rebbe had this deep, true insight that a major tool used by the evil inclination to see to it that this basic issue of the *churban* is not attended to, is to convince people that, unfortunately, they have absolutely no time. Addressing this matter in a realistic, practical manner, the Rebbe's daily spiritual exercise was to sit down and mourn for one single second—how could anybody object to this? I'm sure, therefore, that it would be the Rebbe's wish to have something included here in honor of the *Shechinah* and the holy *Beis HaMikdash*.

This subject of the destruction of the Temple brings the recollection of the Tishah B'Av night I spent with the Rebbe's *minyan*. After *Eichah* I walked home in the Rebbe's company. Such serious emotion emanated from him that I felt that anything that might be said would be out of place. If one was as sincerely connected as he should be to the meaning of this day, there was absolutely nothing that could be said that would be appropriate. So quite understandably, during our walk home the Rebbe was quiet; this atmosphere was transmitted to me, and I likewise was quiet. This was the silent walk.

When we arrived at the Rebbe's home he motioned that I could accompany him upstairs. The house was empty and dark—the family was in the country. Once we were both seated on the living room floor, the Rebbe finally broke the silence. We are living so many years from the *churban*, he said, and it is extremely difficult to relate to it in a realistic manner and actually mourn. On the other hand, the horrifying atrocity that *Klal Yisrael* experienced so recently—the murder and torture of millions of men, women and children—we can, unfortunately, relate to. We must arouse our emotional response to this, the Rebbe said, and superimpose it on the *churban Beis HaMikdash*. The Rebbe then proceeded to recount a selection of the tragic atrocities experienced by *Klal Yisrael* in the Holocaust.

I subsequently heard this precious advice from the Rebbe in the course of many *shiurim*—this technique of stimulating the emotions by transposing the feelings from an area where they are more readily accessible.

In connection with this the Rebbe quoted the story told in the *gemara* of a widow who resided near R' Yochanan. The tragic loss of her husband caused her to weep nightly. The sounds of her sobs echoed through the silence of the Babylonian night. Reaching the ears of the great sage, the grief-ridden cries stimulated him to join her, to cry for the *churban Beis HaMikdash*. Night after night, rivers of tears flowed from his eyes until this brought on such deterioration in his health that it became necessary to find another dwelling place for the widow. As the Rebbe expressed it, R' Yochanan flew on the wings of another's emotion.

In conjunction with this very same important principle and practical tool, the Rebbe demonstrated another, albeit different, application. Sometimes a person who has animosity toward an individual for a wrong which he cannot forgive, discovers that under the influence of wine he has a warm spot in his heart for this person, but hesitates to give in and express this warmth because he feels it is not really truthful. He should flow along and allow himself to be influenced, the Rebbe said. Hashem made this to help us smooth our differences with our fellow man. Hashem even allowed Himself to be influenced by Noach's sacrifices (*Bereishis* 8:21). Perhaps this can help us to explain the fact that Noach gave priority to planting a vineyard. Although Noach is criticized for this, he surely had a significant motive in mind. With the Rebbe's insight we can now offer an explanation: Noach planted the vineyard as a means of evoking warmth among people. This idea seems especially fitting when we consider that the Flood came about because of a lack of love and good feelings among mankind.

The Rebbe once pointed out something which at first glance might seem to contradict the above. He related that occasionally students in the Slabodka Yeshivah became lost in prayer, with tears streaming down their faces. Looking on, the other *bachurim* wondered: was this a yearning for the return of the honor of the *Shechinah* bursting forth, or perhaps mourning for the destruction of the Temple, or a striving to become close to Hashem? The *mash-giach*, however, remarked that the observers should not become overly impressed, for these young men may very possibly be crying because of the patches upon patches on their clothing. (As a side point of interest, the Rebbe elaborated on the dire poverty of the students at that time and their great self-sacrifice for Torah. Owning a pair of pants without patches was unheard of, and the boys actually wore clothing that had been patched on top of the patches.)

The Rebbe explained that a person can actually fool even himself into thinking that his tears are for spiritual yearning, while in reality they are for some materialistic want. Drawing from the idea we presented earlier, it would seem commendable to enlist the emotional response from one area and apply it to another. The difference is that in one case one intentionally transposes his emotions, whereas in a case like that of the weeping *bachur*, a person might mistakenly believe that he is emotionally affected by spirituality when it is really something else that is arousing his feelings.

The Rebbe also opened our eyes to the realization that we are living in an era in which our emotional responses and feelings are at a very low point. Perhaps this is what is meant in the Torah when it says that before the Final Redemption we will have hearts of stone. The Rebbe pointed out the difficulty adults, especially men, have in crying nowadays. Until recently it was acceptable for adults to cry, even in public, for joy or sadness. Today this is unacceptable, a sign of weakness, and something to be ashamed of. The Rebbe cited the assassination of President Kennedy, who tragically bled to death on the lap of his young wife. At the funeral she did not shed a tear, and the headlines stated: "Jacqueline, We Are Proud of You."

The Rebbe pointed out that even at a young age, if a child cries he is often reprimanded by an adult: "I am surprised at you." When a person is overcome with an urge to cry today, said the Rebbe, he makes a beeline for a restroom, so as not to be caught in the act.

In the framework of the *vaadim*, which were private groups that met for character training, the Rebbe actually gave us exercises to stimulate our ability to cry. He related how the famous Rav Herman visited the *Kosel* every single day to pray for the Jews in Russia, and he would not leave the *Kosel* until he had shed one tear on their behalf. The Rebbe told us this to illustrate the difficulty that even Rav Herman seemed to have concerning this matter.

Chazal tell us that the only gateway to the Heavens that is presently open is the gateway of tears. May we be worthy to see the *geulah sheleimah*, complete with "loud walks" and rivers of joyful tears.

CHAPTER FORTY

Big Small Talk

A s I think back to one walk I had with the Rebbe, my first thought is that there isn't much to relate about it. The time was primarily taken up by what people call ordinary small talk. The Rebbe conducted these "small talk walks" with me from time to time, and even on walks when the Rebbe honored me with an inspiring insight into *Mishlei* or a dictum of *Chazal*, ordinary talk was also often included in the agenda. Frequently when we arrived at the Rebbe's home, he would invite me into his private room where he would continue the conversation. He would question me about what was transpiring in my life, from my relationships with various family members to the many aspects of my yeshivah life. He was not satisfied with superficial answers, and in his inquiries he delved into each subject in great detail. And whenever the Rebbe's next opportunity to question me came up, he would continue where we had left off at the previous session, showing how important my seemingly insignificant affairs were to him. For many years, on Shabbos afternoons I attended the Rebbe's *shiur* on the *Aggadata* found in *Shas*. I walked the Rebbe home after Maariv and it became a regular weekly ritual that after *Havdalah* he would invite me into his room for an update of my personal current events. Closing my eyes, I can actually feel myself sitting in the room, with the Rebbe sitting opposite me on a couch, anxiously questioning me.

Of course, I was pleased by the Rebbe's personal interest; it took time, however, until what was happening sank in and I began to understand and appreciate what the Rebbe was doing, and how precious this gift actually was. Just considering the matter in terms of the time it took, I came to realize that the Rebbe must have deliberately scheduled this time for me, for he was scrupulously conscious and careful of how he used every moment. [Later in his life this fact became more apparent when he stopped attending weddings, with the exception of those of his own immediate family members, and even at those he stayed only for a short time, holding his coat on his arm all the while and refusing to put it down.] Besides the time element, there was his heart and concern. And on top of this there was his constant input: the insights, advice, guidance, support, and strengthening when needed. When I considered all that, I realized the staggering extent of the Rebbe's graciousness to me.

There was yet another element present which I want to mention specifically because of its extreme importance. This was the Rebbe's exceptional ability to listen. The Rebbe showed interest, attentiveness, and the simple patience to listen that is so rare today—the ability to pay full attention without interrupting: no comments, no advice, no stories, no sharing of his own scenarios, no guessing what was coming next, no criticism, and no input until I had finished whatever I was telling him. This has special significance in our present generation, for in our times we see extreme weakness in this capacity. In all that concerns the use of the *ear* we can say that we are living an *era* of weakness in this *area*.

It is very common today when one seeks counsel, even from a high-quality person, that they interrupt with their advice even before you have finished supplying the information about the question, which simply does not make any sense. This is unfortunately not an exaggeration, and far from being rare, it is typical. I have heard the cry so often—"I don't have a single person that I can speak to." The tragedy of this is compounded by the unique situation which exists today. We are living in a very unusual time. On the one hand we enjoy the blessings of abundance, plenty, and relative peace. One of the greatest gifts the Rebbe gave us was a realization of the extent of our obligation to recognize the blessings that Hashem bestows upon us. The standard of what is available to us in food, clothing, and shelter is on a tremendously high level. What is so strange, however, is that on the other hand we are also going through very troubling times.

Many are poverty stricken or overtaken by difficult illnesses. Others struggle with *shalom bayis* problems, many of which end in divorce. We see multitudes of single people who cannot find their marriage partners, and every day we hear of more widows, widowers, orphans, and rebellious offspring who forsake Hashem and the Torah. The situation has reached such proportions that if we look around in almost any environment there is hardly a home that is not besieged by at least one of these troubles. All around us, the need for any assistance we can give is great. The need for sensitive ears to listen as the multitude of troubled Jews unburden their heavy hearts is so vital.

Let us be inspired by the example of the Rebbe and open our ears and hearts to the afflicted. May Hashem, the Merciful One, put an end to all our troubles and bring salvation to all.

CHAPTER FORTY-ONE

Cornering in on the "Ketzos"

*R*ebbe, after so many years of escorting you on your walks, I feel especially indebted to Hashem for His *hashgachah pratis* in granting me the *zechus* of accompanying you to your final resting place on *Har HaZeisim*. At your *levayah* I became enlightened about one of the most important and outstanding aspects of your life, something I had never been aware of throughout the long years I knew you.

Today we live in the age of specialization. We have great *talmidei chachamim* who are masters of *Shas*, others who are masters of halachah, others who excel in the depths of *lomdus*—understanding the complex logic of the Torah. We have authorities on *Tanach*, and we have those who serve as leaders in the vast world of *hashkafah*, inspiration, *middos* and *yiras Shamayim*. The Rebbe's domain was his immense knowledge of *Shas, Tanach,* and the world of *Aggadata,* in addition to *hashkafah,* the art of character training, and expertise in inculcating the true values of life.

I never associated the Rebbe with the image of exceptional knowledge of the *Ketzos HaChoshen,* the cornerstone of the world of *lomdus.* So much did my image of the Rebbe deviate from that of the *lomdus* specialist that I would have felt as uncomfortable delving into the *Ketzos* with him as I would feel discussing a subtle thought on character training with one of my *rebbeim* whose primary field was *lomdus.*

And now, at your *levayah,* Rebbe, I made this awesome discovery—you were in fact very familiar indeed with the *Ketzos.* You knew every single one and knew them all by heart; they were completely committed in your memory. This was such an astounding accomplishment that it is incomprehensible to me. It is amazing how I could be so close and have such a strong connection with the Rebbe, and yet not even have begun to comprehend his greatness.

Subsequently, I learned that when the Rebbe parted from his own great Rebbe, *HaRav HaGaon* R' Isaac Sher—who revolutionized the Rebbe's whole life and inspired him to learn in Slabodka—R' Isaac asked what the Rebbe was planning for the future, after his return to the U.S. There was a *talmid* in Slabodka who had achieved the great accomplishment of learning the entire *Ketzos* by heart. The Rebbe replied to R' Isaac's inquiry by uttering that student's name, alluding to the fact that he would strive to reach the same goal. R' Isaac's reply was "*Nu?*" (meaning, "Well, go to it!"). And with that the Rebbe and the *talmid* parted. Eventually, the Rebbe achieved this formidable goal.

Chazal's advice to one who wishes to sharpen his thinking faculties is to pursue the study of monetary laws. The Rebbe certainly was an outstanding manifestation of this, as one could see from his wisdom and sharpness. It is known that R' Moshe Mordechai Epstein devoted an hour a day to the study of the *Ketzos;* it is commonly understood that this was a Torah-study "hobby" of his. I would venture to say that he maintained this *Ketzos* program in order to keep his mind sharp.

The most precious commodity we possess is the clarity of mind to perceive the truths of the world. If one understood how much his mind has to gain through following the advice of *Chazal* to study monetary subjects, we would be so dedicated to this undertaking that we would probably neglect every other obligation.

The Rebbe often said that one of the greatest gifts one can receive from Heaven is to be conscious and mentally alert when about to embark on the great journey to the next world. Likewise, the Rebbe strongly advised careful planning on how to utilize this precious gift if one should be granted it from Heaven. First of all, this opportunity should be used for *teshuvah*, the recital of *Viduy*. Second, at this time one should make his most important and meaningful requests of his family and loved ones. Time, effort, and thought should be invested in planning and rehearsing what he is going to request at this most crucial, valuable time. If one has special ideals and practices which he particularly cherishes and wishes his family to uphold, or specific spiritual dangers which especially concern him and which he would want his family to be aware of and to create a fence to protect themselves from, this is the most potent opportunity to present his requests. It is also a time to engage in Torah study, fulfilling the ideal of learning up until one's last breath.

The Rebbe emphasized strongly the importance of constantly praying to Hashem that one should merit the great opportunity of full mental capacity before leaving this world. There is no question that he himself engaged in these special prayers and that he was granted this request from Heaven.

The Rebbe fulfilled all the above, including an intensive conversation with his son, R' Eliezer, for two hours. With his grandchildren surrounding the bed, close to his final moments, the Rebbe recited from memory a *Ketzos* and then had them repeat it back to him. Rebbe, you were probably one of the select few that the *Ketzos* kept sharp until the end.

CHAPTER FORTY-TWO

Hakaras HaTov

On many of our walks, and likewise in the course of many *shiurim*, the Rebbe greatly emphasized the importance of *hakaras hatov*, gratitude. According to what we see from the Rebbe's own example, it is the single most important element in the service of Hashem. The Rebbe often quoted the *Chovos HaLevavos*, who states that the most pronounced, open declaration ever made by Hashem was the *"Anochi"* of the first of the Ten Commandments. Hashem introduces Himself to us there as our Redeemer from the slavery of Egypt. Wouldn't we have expected that He would present Himself as the Creator of the world? But as the *Chovos HaLevavos* explains, Hashem wanted us to relate to Him as an actual, immediate reality, and since our prime motivation for serving Hashem is our gratitude to Him, we can relate to Him more easily on an immediate level through our gratitude to Him as our Freer from bondage and cruel slavery than as the Creator of the world.

The Rebbe very often quoted Hillel's famous distillation of the whole Torah into a commandment not to do to your fellow anything which you would find objectionable if it were done to you. How this reflects the entire Torah obviously needs explanation. Based on Rashi's commentary that the "fellow" Hillel was referring to is none other than Hashem *yisbarach*, the Rebbe explained as follows: After presenting a friend with a magnificent, valuable gift, followed by making a minor request of him, one would find it very upsetting if he refused. Hashem showers us with countless magnificent, gracious gifts and every commandment revolves around one of these gifts. How, then, can we not acquiesce to Hashem's request?

For example, the Rebbe would explain, if you live under a park bench you do not have to put up a *mezuzah*; if you do not have clothing you do not have to wear *tzitzis*; someone without arms is not required to put on *tefillin*; and there is no mitzvah of *pidyon haben* for someone who does not have a firstborn son. These are actually the words of *Chazal* in *Midrash Rabbah*. It is so clear to me now, Rebbe, why you delved into, taught, wrote about and constantly emphasized *Shaar HaBechinah* in *Chovos HaLevavos*, since in order to have proper gratitude to Hashem one must as a prerequisite study and comprehend the gracious gifts He presented to man through the creation.

Gratitude toward our fellow man is likewise the foundation for successful fulfillment of our obligations toward others. Beyond that, it is also a basic prerequisite for our gratitude to Hashem, for only one who shows his gratitude to his fellow man, who is visible, can have any hope of showing it to Hashem, Who is invisible and intangible.

In the course of many walks and talks, as you discussed this matter of *hakaras hatov*, many aspects at first seemed confusing, making it difficult for me to crystallize precisely what *hakaras hatov* is. After hearing so much from you on the subject and trying to organize it all, I found that three distinct areas emerged, all under the banner of *hakaras hatov*.

Hakaras hatov — recognizing the good intellectually: having a full, in-depth perception and comprehension of the kindness rendered.

Hakaras hatov — recognizing the good emotionally: feeling in the depth of one's heart a suitable degree of gratitude toward the benefactor.

Hakaras hatov — actively showing recognition of the good: demonstrating to the benefactor your recognition and appreciation for the kindness rendered by repaying it in some way.

In analyzing the *hatavah*, the benefit rendered, on the intellectual level, we find it has two parts: the favor itself and the giver. In contemplating the *hatavah* in order to arrive at *hakaras hatov* on this level, one must consider how much he was in need of the benefit, how much he gained by it, and its quality. One must think of how much effort was exerted by the giver and his motivation (even a selfish motivation requires gratitude, although the purer the intention, the greater the gratitude due).

The next step in *hakaras hatov*, recognizing the good, is generating deep feelings of gratitude in one's heart. It would seem natural that once the first step, attaining clear insight, is fulfilled, the feelings should then flow without further effort. However, in actuality, if special effort is not devoted to awakening feelings of gratitude, all that clear recognition of the benefits bestowed will unfortunately have almost no effect.

For example, the gratitude one owes one's parents is so great that there are no words that can describe it and do it justice. If just once we had to wake someone for assistance at 3 A.M. we would be eternally indebted to them; yet our parents have willingly come to our aid hundreds of times at all hours of the night, and it is rare that we even give this a passing thought. Many of us experience a sudden flash of insight in which we are overcome with an awareness of at least part of what our parents did for us. These are feelings of tremendous awe that humble us as all at once we comprehend their years of selfless devotion and dedication—the countless times they pulled their weary bodies out of bed to care for us; the frantic, nerve-shattering trips to the emergency room; the bone-chilling fears; and the oceans of tears.

We cannot depend on these spontaneous enlightenments, which are gifts from Heaven, for our feelings of gratitude, but at least they serve as a model for how we should be feeling. To maintain the proper level of feeling we must repeatedly reawaken ourselves.

Another example is the blindness of husbands to the constant acts of kindness bestowed on them by their wives. A wife typically buys the food, cooks it, rarely serves the same thing twice in a row, washes, dries, irons, and folds the laundry, takes care of the house, makes an effort to look nice for her husband ... the list goes on and on. If a man were to contemplate this for even a moment, he would realize how much gratitude he owes his wife for everything that she does for him.

The third component of gratitude is repaying the good that was done for us. This can be manifested in three ways: through thought, speech, and action. Sometimes the favor is repaid in an active way and sometimes in a passive way. Repayment may be immediate or over an extended period of time. Sometimes the favor is repaid to the benefactor and sometimes to his extended family.

Gratitude in thought means cultivating feelings of appreciation toward your benefactors for the good that they have done for you. It means liking them or loving them and regarding them positively. It will also be reflected in your readiness to judge them favorably, even when they do you an injustice. It should be easier for you to overcome any negative feelings toward them, because of the favor they did. Even in a situation where you are not required to judge them favorably, you will still go to great lengths to do so if you are grateful. And if you cannot even judge them favorably, you will at any rate forgive them because of the gratitude you feel. These are a few examples of how one might reward a benefactor and show him gratitude through thought.

Showing gratitude through speech has two aspects:

1. Get into the habit of voicing brief expressions of appreciation frequently. For example, if you're a married man, make sure you thank your wife for all the different things that she does for you. If she sews a button on your shirt, she deserves to be thanked for this—do not take it for granted.

2. There are times when it is appropriate to be more elaborate in expressing feelings of gratitude for the good that a person does for you. For example, sit down once in a while and tell your wife how much you appreciate everything she does. A phenomenon that has puzzled me—and in which I have invested a lot of time and energy trying to understand it—is the difficulty many men have in expressing gratitude to their wives. This seems to be a general, widespread problem and can affect even those who truly understand, recognize, and feel to a full extent the gratitude they owe to their wives. Despite their awareness, they are faced with difficulty in expressing their gratitude. Nevertheless, one should make his best effort to do so.

The third way of expressing gratitude is through actions. Do things to make your benefactor happy. To continue with our example of one's wife as benefactor, these gestures can be small, such as buying flowers, or major expressions of thanks, such as expensive gifts, or investments of time and effort, such as helping your wife around the house (which the husband should do anyway, but sometimes does as a show of gratitude).

It is extremely important for a person to think of ways to make his spouse happy. This necessitates developing the skill of considering other people's needs, and what gives them pleasure. Sometimes it is important when giving a gift to make your gratitude known to the recipient, because what is most significant in the gesture is the emotions that accompany the gift. Many times a person gives a gift only because he feels that he has to, but it doesn't really come from his heart. A wife can sense this. But at least if the husband says something, offers some verbal expression of gratitude, it will make a difference.

Another form of gratitude can be called "passive." This may be seen in a person's readiness to avoid or defuse an argument. Sometimes a person quarrels with his spouse and thinks of something really hurtful to say. But at that moment, he thinks of how much he really owes her for everything she does for him, and instead of coming out with that hurtful remark, he keeps silent and even apologizes—even though he still feels that he is right. He holds himself back because of his gratitude.

Sometimes, depending upon the importance of the favor, it is appropriate for the recipient's entire family to show gratitude to the family of the benefactor. At times, this obligation may even extend over many generations, even after the death of the benefactor himself.

Rebbe, the gratitude we owe you just for this one tremendous favor of teaching us gratitude is infinite. Let us contemplate the various aspects of this *hatavah*:

Q. Do we need it?
A. As much as our breath.
Q. The quality of the benefit?
A. Couldn't be better.
Q. How much did we gain?
A. It is life itself.
Q. How might we express our gratitude in a more elaborate form?
A. It would take "miles and miles."

CHAPTER FORTY-THREE

A Seder for the Seder

O ne day in early spring while walking with the Rebbe, I took the opportunity to discuss a pressing issue with him. Pesach was drawing near and I was faced with a great dilemma. In my family the Pesach Seder was one of the most important functions on the calendar. All the family members—including aunts, uncles, and cousins—came together for a united celebration of the gala event.

At the same time, in the Mirrer Yeshivah, which I had recently joined, the *"olam"* was discussing the importance of attending the Seder of an *adam gadol*, claiming it was vital that one should take advantage of the opportunity, while still single, of witnessing the Seder of a *talmid chacham*. After marriage this opportunity is usually not feasible, they claimed, and besides, one who witnesses such a Seder gains precious insight and knowledge on how to conduct his own Seder when the time comes. The *"olam"* felt that this learning experience was a preparation for leading one's own family and students during one's entire future life, and therefore it took priority over family obligations and feelings. I, too, was pressed by the question: if I should go to the Seder of a *talmid chacham*, which one should I choose, and how was I going to get myself invited there? On the other hand, what about my family? Was it really right for me to desert them after such a long tradition of being together for the Seder?

After I presented both sides of the issue to the Rebbe as clearly as I could, he said something I didn't expect, and I was indeed shocked. The Rebbe answered with a personal invitation to me to join him at his own Pesach Seder. As it turned out, there was something I had never known. The Rebbe always had two single boys as Seder guests. Once they were chosen, these boys had the *zechus* of coming every year until they married. The *bachurim* who had most recently enjoyed this privilege of attending the Rebbe's Seder had married during the course of that past year, so I was invited to fill one of these vacancies.

To merit sitting at the Rebbe's Seder table was something of which I had never dreamed I would be found worthy. But it actually came to reality, and I had the *zechus* of attending the Rebbe's Seder for a number of years until my own wedding. The purpose and goal was certainly accomplished: witnessing and participating in a Seder which served as a model for the future. This happened around the year 1958 and to this very day I draw from these Sedarim.

The grand night of the Seder finally arrived, and I was in for a big surprise, which turned out to be my greatest enlightenment of the evening. One of the Rebbe's greatest fortes was the subject of *yetzias Mitzrayim*, since it is the foremost source of *emunah* and gratitude to Hashem. The Rebbe frequently elaborated on this subject. So I was tingling with anticipation: what would the Rebbe have to say on this night of nights, when we commemorate *yetzias Mitzrayim*? Surely there would be mountains of insights and explanations. I was actually going to be at the table of the king of "*sipur yetzias Mitzrayim*" as he sat on his throne that night. It was surely going to be the "Super

Seder." Imagine my shock as I watched the Rebbe "shooting" through the Seder—with none of the great elaborations or extensive explanations that I had been expecting.

What I was actually witnessing was an example of what a Seder is really supposed to be according to the true framework of *Chazal*, who geared the Seder for the participation and appreciation of the children and centered its dynamics on holding their attention.

The Rebbe's reading of the story of *yetzias Mitzrayim* was fast moving, but he took enough time for a clear explanation of the basic ideas, along with many additional short insights dispersed throughout the Seder. (In the chapter *"Parlez-vous Yiddish?"* I quoted one of the little treasures the Rebbe said at the Seder table.) The elaborations were saved for after the completion of the Haggadah: speaking in detail of *yetzias Mitzrayim* until overtaken by sleep, which the Rebbe fulfilled exactly as prescribed by *Chazal*.

Who could have been a more appropriate person to ask my Seder *shailah* than the Rebbe? This was an opportunity I simply couldn't "pass over."

CHAPTER FORTY-FOUR

All for the Boss

*W*e were completely soaked with perspiration, sapped of all energy, hoarse and ready to collapse: the Rebbe, one or two close *talmidim*, and myself. We had just finished the nighttime *hakafos* of Simchas Torah. The Rebbe, as usual, had expended a lot of energy into creating a real Simchas Torah spirit, personally leading the singing and dancing for hours, with a few of his close disciples assisting him all the way. It was vital to have them rally round and help to imbue the *hakafos* with the proper spirit of joy and elevation since the *baalei batim* were not accustomed to celebrating Simchas Torah in this manner (as we explained in the chapter on the Rugby *kehillah*).

The members of the congregation had departed, and we were just starting on our way home together when the Rebbe called us back to the now completely deserted shul. The lights had been automatically switched off, leaving just the eerie glow that emanated from the *ner tamid*. The Rebbe then requested that we form a circle and join him in song and dance. What could this be all about? This chapter could have been called "the walk that turned into a dance."

Many times the Rebbe depicted the scenario of a sincere Jew spiritedly dancing at a wedding or on Simchas Torah. He pauses for a moment for introspection, a true-to-heart spiritual inventory. "Who am I kidding?" he says to himself. "Let's face it, I am aware of all the eyes that are focused upon my great dancing skills. Am I really dancing to make the *chasan* happy? Am I dancing in honor of Hashem and His Torah, or is this for my honor, my pride, or perhaps so that someone watching will take a keen interest in me for a *shidduch*? What's the point of this false act, anyway?" And with that he abandons the circle of dancers.

The Rebbe's comment on this was that most people do not bother to delve into their motives. Then there are those who do but deceive themselves with self-righteousness and don't suspect any selfish motive. Between the non-carers and the self-deceivers we find the on-target righteous who back down, feeling that they have the wrong motives. The Rebbe pointed out that these pious abstainers are mistaken. He quoted the *gemara* in *Pesachim* which speculates as to why in the process of *bedikas chametz* a person should refrain from placing his hand where he may be hurt. He should be covered by the general protection that the Torah promises to one who is occupied in performing a mitzvah—why, then, should he need to be concerned about where he puts his hand while searching for *chametz* on Erev Pesach? The *gemara* then suggests that perhaps besides looking for the *chametz*, a person might simultaneously be searching for an object he has lost. On this the *gemara* declares that even if it were so, the searcher would still be protected, for performing a mitzvah with dual intention does not nullify his good intention. The *gemara* emphatically declares that one who does a mitzvah for combined interests, for the sake of Heaven and for his own personal motives, can still be considered a pious person. (The *gemara* concludes that the reason one does not search in dangerous places is because we fear he will seek his personal effects only after completing his search for *chametz*, when he is no longer afforded the protection of a *sheliach mitzvah*.)

The Rebbe emphasized that the principle pronounced in the *gemara* here has awesome implications in our daily lives. We can address our pious friend who deserts the dancing either for the *chasan* and *kallah* or for Simchas Torah because he suspects himself of personal motives: You are surely dancing in honor of Hashem and the Torah; you surely want to bring joy to the *chasan* and *kallah*; this pride that concerns you is at worst considered compound intentions. It is in just such an instance that the *gemara* condones the dual intentions and declares the individual righteous. On the other hand, one should not refrain from applying one's positive intention of doing a mitzvah for the sake of Heaven on the grounds that because he is aware of having an ulterior motive, he feels it is false, hypocritical, and pointless to attribute lofty, idealistic intentions to his act as well. The Rebbe pointed out that the *gemara* is shouting to us that we surely should implement these good thoughts and that by no means are they lost despite an admixture of personal motives.

This now opens a whole new horizon of thought and new worlds that can have a great impact on our daily lives. Many of our occupations involve *chesed*—various acts of kindness. Take a physician for example; because he maintains his practice for a livelihood, this is often his only intent. But as the Rebbe explained, based on the principle derived from the *gemara* of the legitimacy of dual intentions, a doctor can incorporate the intention of kindness into the care he gives his patients despite the monetary aspect of his practice. The Rebbe then said that another unique application would be the bus driver—what kindness! When this profession is contemplated objectively one can surely see the magnificent act of kindness in driving a multitude of individuals to their destinations daily. A driver who harnesses his mental powers to work for "the sake of Heaven" could become a spiritual multi-millionaire.

Once thinking along these lines it is hard to find a livelihood not connected with acts of kindness on some level. Working to support a family is itself a *chesed*, and thus it is always connected to a mitzvah.

The Rebbe then changed the focus of this matter of *l'shem Shamayim* to our normal daily life. He pointed out how every single thing we do can potentially be directed to the service of Hashem. Most of us, upon hearing this, would say that this is living on a lofty level reserved only for *tzaddikim*, *mekubalim*, and *talmidei chachamim*. This would be true if the intent of serving Hashem had to be the only thought permeating every act. However, we can again make use of the ruling on dual intentions from the *gemara* in *Pesachim*, this time, applying it to everything we do. Whatever personal intentions we may have in all our endeavors, we are always capable of slipping in a thought directing it to the service of Hashem.

One of the greatest factors that deter us from this great opportunity to dedicate all our actions to Hashem is the feeling that our feeble, measly, fleeting thoughts cannot accomplish this. The Rebbe uprooted this inaccuracy, mainly through the *vaadim*, and inspired us with the ambition to grow in this vast frontier of the thoughts attached to our acts.

Some of the thoughts the Rebbe suggested that we might adopt to accompany our acts were from *Chazal*. For example, the *gemara* states that washing one's face is like caring for the statue of the king, since we are created in the *tzelem Elokim*. When shining our shoes we are fulfilling the mitzvah of sanctifying the Name of Hashem in public. Brushing our teeth is fulfilling the commandment of caring for our body. When making our Shabbos preparations—showering, grooming, shopping, and cooking—we should remember to think specifically of the mitzvah of preparing for Shabbos.

Despite the Rebbe's heroic efforts to enlighten, motivate and inspire us to implement dual intentions, he made sure that we retained the perspective that the ultimate goal is pure, unadulterated intention *l'shem Shamayim*.

The Rebbe explained that our dancing in the course of the evening had been wonderful, but he wanted one little dance without any honor or pride. So here we have a little dance — All for the Boss.

CHAPTER FORTY-FIVE

The Walks Live On

Dear Rebbe, I'm here from *Eretz Yisrael*, on one of my infrequent, brief visits to the States. Not having seen you for so many years, I wanted to meet with you and perhaps discuss some personal matters. You invite me to join you on a walk! "Meet me on Friday afternoon at my son's yeshivah, after I finish the *vaad*." I arrive at our meeting place, and just from the sight of you I sense the presence of the *Shechinah*. I am startled to see how you look, how little effect aging has had on your physical appearance. This is something I have been noticing all through the years, but not having seen you in such a span of time, now it is really very outstanding. This phenomenon perfectly reflects the complete panorama of vital foundations of thought and living with which you constantly strive to inspire the world. These are phenomenal recipes which breed joy into your life and happiness into your thoughts. This is the absolute formula for preserving youth, and you are the supreme example.

And now we set out on our walk. What words can describe the feeling of elation to once again be in your physical presence and actually walk side by side with you? That supreme feeling of ecstasy makes my memory of the experience a little blurry, but I will try my best to recall it.

We must have started off by discussing the important matter that served as my excuse for making the appointment. Whatever it was, it did not take too long to get your input and we were done with the matter. We probably passed a billboard proudly proclaiming the seventy-five flavors of Howard Johnson's ice cream which brought you to a detailed review of the subject. To you this is extremely significant, since it represents and symbolizes the marvelous era of blessings of plenty from Hashem in which we are currently living. You were not in any way encouraging indulgence in this massive display of materialism. It was just for the purpose of taking note and being filled with awe at Hashem's blessings.

Shortly afterward we passed a fruit and vegetable store, and you got right into discussing the merchandise on display, admiring in detail all the aspects of physical beauty in the various kinds of produce, and then the concert of their variety of tastes. You exhibited your perpetual awe at the downpour of blessings, at the panorama of plenty that Hashem has made available to us, which was displayed at the store. As you cleverly pointed out, even if one did not indulge in any purchases from this luscious array of fruits and vegetables, just knowing that we have such blessings available is an unexpected and unrecognized enjoyment in itself.

The most wondrous part of this is that in those glorious past years, on so many of our walks you pointed this out, and now you address it as if it were a brand new insight that never occurred to you before. Likewise, now our walk brings us past a beautiful garden, and with the same fresh enthusiasm as you showed in the old days, you verbally pluck the pretty petals of the tulips, violets, and roses. You do not fail to point out the senselessness of the general populace in feeling they have to own and work the garden for themselves in order to truly appreciate the flora.

"Rebbe, Rebbe, where are you?" I ask, suddenly realizing that I have lost you. Then I am quick to discover that you are indeed by my side, but bent over. You rise and you clasp in your hand some "gems." "One who can really appreciate seashells is richer than the greatest millionaire." If this wise old saying applies to anyone, it must surely be you. You now have in your possession an array of seed-carrying vehicles. Blowing on one downy-looking sample, you demonstrate how the puffs are airborne, each with its precious parcel consisting of a seed, each one transporting its package to produce a new generation of splendid growth. You admire the magnificent engineering feat of how the puffs are designed to float in the air and are mobilized by the slightest breeze.

Another specimen near the top of your hit parade is the amazing little parachutes which, after being ejected into the air, gracefully float with the seed, the package dangling from this actual, miniature parachute, another major engineering feat. We then turn to the next of your favorites—the propellers. These marvelous, precisely shaped propellers that spin perfectly in the wind carry their precious seed package. If I recall correctly, these were always the dearest to you.

Your deep appreciation and awe for all these things were those of a *gadol hador*, but your excitement was as sweet and fresh as that of an innocent young child making the discovery for the very first time. Your enthusiasm spills over as if this were your first exposure to these wonders.

Years later I discovered a phenomenon in *Eretz Yisrael* to which I reacted with an excitement that was a pure reflection of your training. It was a low plant that grows green, fuzzy, oval balls about three quarters of an inch in length. When it reaches a certain stage of growth and is touched, the "football" detaches itself from the plant and flies into the air, spraying a waterlike liquid all around, especially on the unwitting victim who touched it. It contains seeds which are distributed in this manner. It is just amazing—I am sure, Rebbe, that had you seen it, it would have been the number one float in your hit parade.

On one of the occasions that I had the *zechus* of sitting at your festive table, we were about to *bentsch*, and you related an episode concerning a *talmid chacham* from a small town. Planning to marry off a child, he was short of funds, and leaving his family, he set out for the central city of Vilna to raise some money. Upon arriving at this magnificent city, one of the greatest Torah centers of the world, the home and headquarters of the Vilna Gaon, he was taken by surprise and became totally enraptured by a *chiddush* in the following halachah: Upon hearing *bentching* recited aloud one must answer "*Amen*" after "*al yechasreinu.*" This *talmid chacham* was so overcome with excitement concerning this *chiddush* that he completely forgot the original purpose of his trip and spent the remainder of his stay in Vilna delving into the depths of this new insight and engaging in discussions on the subject, oblivious to his financial burden and obligation. Upon returning home he was beaming with the excitement of the "treasure" he had brought from Vilna and instructed his anxious family to set the table for a *seudah*. After completing the meal the family *bentsched* and when "*al yechasreinu*" was reached—he called out, full of joy, "*A-M-E-N!*"

In the course of our special walk you brought to my attention a new insight regarding sensitivity toward our fellow man. It was so outstanding to me that it almost overshadowed everything else in our walk, as in the Vilna episode above. I do not recall your ever mentioning this before and I myself never thought of it on my own. As we were walking together the number of people coming toward us from the opposite direction increased dramatically, whereupon you puzzlingly requested that we switch to walking single file. When the density of the crowd coming toward us thinned out, you signaled that we could resume walking side by side. When questioned about this unusual request, you explained that walking side by side causes a crowd of people coming in the opposite direction the extra bother of walking around us. You argued, why should they be required to walk around us just because we want to walk together? You brought to my attention that it was not only one set of people coming our way, but a multitude, all having to go out of their way in order for us to keep together. This is a significant new insight. Sometimes a group of four, five, or six walks abreast and the bother imposed is much greater, since everyone is forced to go around the edges. Often, we are the victims of this and find it bothersome and annoying. The idea, once known, is really very simple, but it took your wisdom, sensitivity, and insight to reveal it.

In truth the appropriate name for this chapter, and this walk, should be along the lines of "*acharon acharon chaviv*"—the last and the sweetest, or "our final walk together." But my heart won't allow it—"The Walks Live On."

After an hour of this Utopia we arrive at Ocean Parkway, and you communicate to me that we are approaching the windup of our rendezvous. After exchanging blessings and acknowledgments, I make a request that we do this again. You laugh and explain that it has been a while since you have engaged in this activity of conversation and walking simultaneously; you find the walking and talking together too strenuous. What we did together today, you explain, was a special, one-time exception you made in my honor for old times' sake. Not knowing that this was the last time I was to merit basking in your presence in this world, I thanked you and we parted, with a big smile still lingering on your face.

An Epilogue

One of the most important insights I gained from the Rebbe was the principle of "this for that"—any invest-ment in a spiritual endeavor, any input of energy, time, or money, always produces returns for us in this world in the form of blessings in the very same spiritual area. It might come immediately or after the passage of many years. This phenomenon is something I am sure we all have experienced and to which we can attest. One puts himself out, making great effort to erect a measly little *succah* and finds that years later he is blessed with the biggest *succah* imaginable.

I find myself today, Rosh Chodesh Iyar, 2001, walking alongside of you, Rebbe, but this time I am accompanying you on the last lap of the walk to your resting place on *Har HaZeisim*, here in Yerushalayim. I feel I was found worthy to do this for the great value, importance, and priority I assigned, and at times the great effort I invested, in our memorable walks together in the past.

On my visits to the *Kosel HaMaaravi* I am able to see in the dis-tance your place on *Har HaZeisim*, and as I gaze at the spot, I try to connect with your *neshamah*, which we hope in the near future, through *techiyas hameisim*, will shine for us again.

$\mathcal{A}$ $\mathcal{T}$ribute

This is a tribute to an old friend, a humble, non-assuming yet outstanding *talmid* of the Rebbe, Rabbi Eliezer Hamburger *shlita*. In our early years we worked together to understand, appreciate and internalize what we learned from our great teacher. May he have the *nachas* of seeing his own progeny continuing in the ways of the Rebbe.

Glossary

Amidah – Shemoneh Esrei

avinu – our father – used in regard to the Patriarchs and G-d

avodah – service

avodas Hashem – service of G-d

baalei batim – laymen, heads of households

bachur (pl. bachurim) – unmarried young man, here a student

bakshu rachamim sign – sign asking people to beseech Heaven for mercy and compassion

bein hazmanim – break between (school) terms; intercession

beis midrash – study hall, usually for Talmudic study

bekius – familiarity, vast knowledge

ben Torah (pl. bnei Torah) – one who studies and observes the teachings of the Torah; an observant Jew; a yeshivah student

bentsch – recite Grace After Meals

berachah – blessing

blatt – folio page (of Talmud)

bnei aliyah – spiritually gifted or accomplished people or people aspiring to spiritual heights

chas v'shalom – Heaven forbid

chasunah (pl. chasunos) – wedding

Chazal – acronym for our Sages of blessed memory

chazaras hashatz – chazzan's repetition of the Amidah

cherem – ban of excommunication

chesed – act of lovingkindness

chiddushim – original Torah insights

chinuch – education

chizuk – encouragement

Chumash (pl. Chumashim) – Five Books of Moses

daf – page (of Talmud)

davening – (v) praying; (n) the prayer service

dayan – judge

derashah – sermon or discourse

derech (lit. path) – manner, approach

Devarim – Deuteronomy

divrei emes – words of truth

emes – truth

emunah – faith, belief in G-d

Eretz Yisrael – Land of Israel

frum (Yid.) – religious, Torah observant

frumkeit (Yid.) – adherence to religious practices

gabbai – synagogue sexton; attendant of a Rebbe

gadol hador – spiritual leader of the generation; a prime Torah leader

galus – exile, Diaspora

Gan Eden – Paradise

gashmiyus – materialism

geshem – rain

hagaon hakadosh – "the holy scholar"

hakafos – on Simchas Torah, the dancing around the readers' table in the synagogue while carrying the Torah scrolls

hakaras hatov – showing gratitude for a benefit received

hashgachas Hashem – Divine providence

hashkafah (pl. hashkafos) – Jewish philosophy; worldview

hasmadah – devoting every available moment to Torah study; diligence and consistency

hatzlachah – success

hilchos bri'us – laws relating to health

ir miklat – city of refuge

iyun – delving in depth

iyun shiur – an in-depth lecture

kavannah – intent, concentration

kehillah – community, congregation

kevod melachim – royal honor

kevod Shamayim – honor of G-d, Divine glory

kinyan – acquisition

kiruv rechokim – drawing near those who are distant from religion

Klal Yisrael – the Jewish people

Kosel – Western Wall

lashon hakodesh – the Holy Tongue, Hebrew

levayah – funeral

Maariv – evening prayer service

machlokes – dispute

maggid shiur – Torah lecturer

manhigim – leaders

masechta – tractate of the Talmud

mashgiach – spiritual dean of a yeshivah

masmid – exceptionally diligent Torah student

me'ein Olam Haba – a taste of the World to
Come

mechilah – forgiveness

mekubal (pl. mekubalim) – mystic; those
who study Kabbalah

melachah – labor forbidden on the Sabbath
by Torah law

Melave Malka – meal eaten Saturday night to
honor the departed Sabbath Queen

mesader kiddushin – one who officiates at a
wedding ceremony

middah – characteristic

Minchah – afternoon prayer service

Mishlei – Proverbs

mispallel – to pray; one who prays

mizrach – east – the direction we face when
we pray; east is the direction in which
Jerusalem is found

Mori V'Rebi – My teacher and my Rebbi

mussar – ethical teachings

ner tamid – eternal light in the synagogue;
light which is never put out

niggun – tune, melody

olam - lit. world; group of people

Olam Haba – the World to Come; a designa-
tion for the eternal afterlife

pasuk – a verse of Scripture

perishus – self-abnegation

pilpul – fine-honed halachic debate

Rebi U'Mori – My Rebbi and my teacher

refuah sheleimah – complete recovery

Ribono Shel Olam – Master of the World; i.e.
G-d

rosh yeshivah (pl. roshei yeshivah) – dean of
a Torah institution

ruach hakodesh – Divine spirit or inspiration

ruchniyus – spirituality

sefarim – books, esp. on learned topics

seudah shelishis – the third Sabbath meal

shadchan – one who arranges marriage
matches

Shas – Talmud

shemiras einyaim – guarding one's eyes from
improper sights

shemiras Shabbos – observance of the
Sabbath

shidduch – marriage match

shitos – opinions

shiur (pl. shiurim) – lecture on a Torah subject

shivah – week of mourning observed after
death of a close relative

shmuessen – ethical discourses

simchas hachaim – joy of living

siyata d'Shmaya – providential aid from G-d

taharah – ritual purification of a dead body

talmid (pl. talmidim) – student

talmid chacham – Torah scholar

tefillah (pl. tefillos) – prayer

teshuvah – repentance

timtum halev – a spiritual "hardening of the
heart" which prevents spiritual growth and
achievement

tzibbur – congregation

vaadim – groups that meet for spiritual
training

Viduy – confession recited before death (and
on Yom Kippur)

yeshivah mahn – an adult who attends a
yeshivah for advanced studies

yesodei hadas – basic foundations of Judaism
or princples of faith

yiras hakavod – respectful awe

yiras Shamayim – fear of heaven

yisbarach – He should be blessed

zocheh – worthy

zt"l – acronym for "zecher tzaddik
livrachah," may the tzaddik's memory be
for a blessing

לעילוי נשמת

Manne	ר' דוב ב"ר שמואל ז"ל
Feilenberg	ר' יעקב מאיר ב"ר אביגדור ז"ל
Feilenberg	מרת חיה פייגל בת ר' ניסן ז"ל
Feilenberg	ר' משה ב"ר יעקב מאיר ז"ל
Manne	ר' שמואל ב"ר דוב ז"ל
Manne	מרת פריידל בת ר' יעקב מאיר ז"ל
Mostofsky	ר' משה ב"ר וועלוועל חיים ז"ל
Mostofsky	מרת דבורה מנוחה ב"ר אברהם שלום ע"ה
Dolinsky	ר' שמואל דוב ב"ר מרדכי ז"ל
Dolinsky	מרת אסתר ריווא ב"ר משה ע"ה
Young	ר' יצחק יוסף ב"ר אברהם צבי ז"ל
Young	ר' חיים ב"ר יצחק יוסף ז"ל
Young	מרת חיה ב"ר אלעזר זאב ז"ל
Lew	מרת יענטא ב"ר חיים ז"ל
Lew	ר' דוד ב"ר פנחס ז"ל
Tisser	ר' יששכר ב"ר מנחם פנחס ז"ל
Antosofsky	לאה אסתר ע"ה בת ר' מרדכי
Paisner	ר' אברהם שלום ב"ר דוב בער ז"ל
Dolinsky	ר' ליפמן ב"ר שמואל דוב ז"ל
Paisner	מרת דבורה מנוחה ב"ר שמואל דוב ע"ה
Young	מרת חוה בר ר' משה ע"ה
Newmark	מרת אסתר ב"ר מנחם מענדל ע"ה
Newmark	ר' יעקב איסר ב"ר שלמה ז"ל
Newmark	ר' יוסף ב"ר יעקב איסר ז"ל
Newmark	ר' משה ב"ר יעקב איסר ז"ל

This volume is part of
THE ARTSCROLL SERIES®
an ongoing project of
translations, commentaries and expositions
on Scripture, Mishnah, Talmud, Halachah,
liturgy, history, the classic Rabbinic writings,
biographies and thought.

For a brochure of current publications
visit your local Hebrew bookseller
or contact the publisher:

Mesorah Publications, ltd

4401 Second Avenue
Brooklyn, New York 11232
(718) 921-9000
www.artscroll.com